… **8**

STUDY GUIDE

Russia and the Soviet Union, 1905–24

Edexcel - IGCSE

app available

www.GCSEHistory.com

CLEVER Lili

Published by Clever Lili Limited.

contact@cleverlili.com

First published 2020

ISBN 978-1-913887-07-0

Copyright notice

All rights reserved. No part of this publication may be reproduced in any form or by any means (including photocopying or storing it in any medium by electronic means and whether or not transiently or incidentally to some other use of this publication) with the written permission of the copyright owner. Applications for the copyright owner's written permission should be addressed to the publisher.

Clever Lili has made every effort to contact copyright holders for permission for the use of copyright material. We will be happy, upon notification, to rectify any errors or omissions and include any appropriate rectifications in future editions.

Cover by: Malchev on Adobe Stock

Icons by: flaticon and freepik

Contributors: Lynn Harkin, Petia Hak

Edited by Paul Connolly and Rebecca Parsley

Design by Evgeni Veskov and Will Fox

All rights reserved

www.GCSEHistory.com

DISCOVER MORE OF OUR IGCSE HISTORY STUDY GUIDES
GCSEHistory.com and Clever Lili

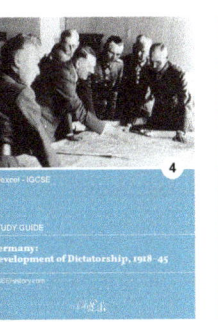

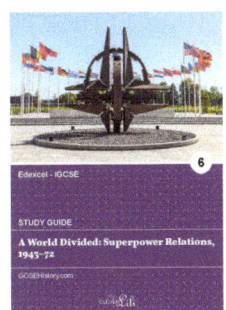

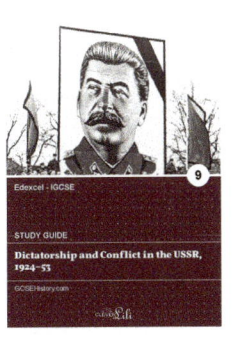

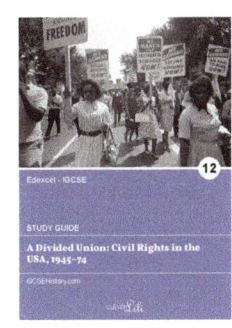

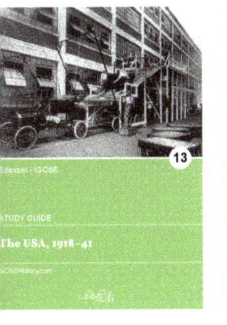

- Germany: Development of Dictatorship, 1918–45
- A World Divided: Superpower Relations, 1943–72
- Dictatorship and Conflict in the USSR, 1924–53
- The Origins and Course of the First World War, 1905–18
- The Vietnam Conflict, 1945–75
- A Divided Union: Civil Rights in the USA, 1945–74
- The USA, 1918–41
- Changes in Medicine, c1848–c1948
- China: Conflict, Crisis and Change, 1900–89

THE GUIDES ARE EVEN BETTER WITH OUR GCSE/IGCSE HISTORY WEBSITE APP AND MOBILE APP

GCSE History is a text and voice web and mobile app that allows you to easily revise for your GCSE/IGCSE exams wherever you are - it's like having your own personal GCSE history tutor. Whether you're at home or on the bus, GCSE History provides you with thousands of convenient bite-sized facts to help you pass your exams with flying colours. We cover all topics - with more than 120,000 questions - across the Edexcel, AQA and CIE exam boards.

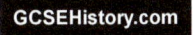

GCSEHistory.com | GET IT ON Google Play | Download on the App Store

Contents

How to use this book 6
What is this book about? 7
Revision suggestions 9

Timelines
Russia and the Soviet Union, 1905-24 13

Background to Russia
Introduction to Russia in the Early 1900s 16
The Russian Calendar 18

How did the Tsars Rule Russia?
Tsarist Rule 19
Tsar Nicholas II 20
Tsarist Police State 22

Discontent
Discontent 23
Political Opposition to the Tsar 24

Causes and Events of 1905 Revolution
The Russo-Japanese War, 1904-05 25
Bloody Sunday, 1905 26
The 1905 Revolution 27

Political Parties
The Octobrist Party 29
The Socialist Revolutionary Party 30
The Trudovik Party 30
The Kadets 31
The Social Democratic Party 32
The Bolshevik Party 32
The Mensheviks 33

Tsar Nicholas II Response
The October Manifesto, 1905 34
The Fundamental Laws 1906 35

The State Duma
The State Duma 36
First Duma, 1906 36
Second Duma, 1907 37
Third Duma, 1907 to 1912 38
Fourth Duma, 1912 to 1917 39
Pyotr (Peter) Stolypin 40
Land Reform 41
Russification 42
The Lena Goldfield Strike, 1912 43

Russia in the First World War
Russia and the First World War 44
Effects of the First World War 46

The February Revolution and the Provisional Government
The February Revolution, 1917 47
The Petrograd Soviet 49
The Provisional Government 50
The June Offensive, 1917 52
The July Days, 1917 53
The Kornilov Revolt, 1917 54
Growth in Support for Bolshevik Party 55

The October Revolution, 1917
The October Revolution, 1917 56
Storming the Winter Palace, October 1917 57

The Bolshevik Consolidation of Power, 1917-18
Bolshevik Consolidation of Power 57
Decree on Land, 1917 59
Decree on Peace, 1917 59
Decree on Workers' Rights, 1917 60
Decree on Nationalities, 1917 61
Declaration of the Rights of the Peoples of Russia, 1917 ... 62
The Constituent Assembly, 1918 62
The Treaty of Brest-Litovsk, March 1918 63
The Communist Party, 1918 64

The Russian Civil War
The Civil War, 1918-1921 65
The Red Terror 67
The Kronstadt Mutiny, 1921 68
The Sovnarkom 70
The Politburo 70

Economic Policies, 1918 to 1928
War Communism, 1918-1921 71
New Economic Policy, 1921-1924 73

People of Russia and the Soviet Union
Tsarina Alexandra 75
Alexander Kerensky 75
General Kornilov 76
Vladimir Lenin 77
Prince Lvov 79
Grigori Rasputin 80
Leon Trotsky 81

Quizzes, amazing exam preparation tools and more at GCSEHistory.com

Glossary 83

Index 87

HOW TO USE THIS BOOK

In this study guide, you will see a series of icons, highlighted words and page references. The key below will help you quickly establish what these mean and where to go for more information.

Icons

WHAT questions cover the key events and themes.

WHO questions cover the key people involved.

WHEN questions cover the timings of key events.

WHERE questions cover the locations of key moments.

WHY questions cover the reasons behind key events.

HOW questions take a closer look at the way in which events, situations and trends occur.

IMPORTANCE questions take a closer look at the significance of events, situations, and recurrent trends and themes.

DECISIONS questions take a closer look at choices made at events and situations during this era.

Highlighted words

Abdicate - occasionally, you will see certain words highlighted within an answer. This means that, if you need it, you'll find an explanation of the word or phrase in the glossary which starts on **page 83**.

Page references

Tudor *(p.7)* - occasionally, a certain subject within an answer is covered in more depth on a different page. If you'd like to learn more about it, you can go directly to the page indicated.

WHAT IS THIS BOOK ABOUT?

Russia and the Soviet Union, 1905-24 is the historical investigation that studies why and how Russia was transformed from an autocratic tsarist government to a communist dictatorship between 1905 and 1924. You will focus on crucial events during this period and study the different social, cultural, political, economic, military and religious changes that occurred.

Purpose
This study will help you understand the complexities and challenges that Tsar Nicholas II faced during his rule. You will investigate themes such as power, law and order, government, revolution, communism, dictatorship, religion, and economy and society. It will enable you to develop the historical skills of identifying key features of a time period and encourage you to analyse and compare sources and evaluate interpretations.

Topics
Russia and the Soviet Union, 1905-24 is split into 5 key enquiries:

- Enquiry 1 looks at the tsarist rule in Russia between 1905 and 1914. You will study how the tsars ruled Russia and the reasons for discontent. You will investigate to what extent Nicholas II was able to successfully deal with this in the years before the First World War.
- Enquiry 2 looks at opposition to Tsar Nicholas II's rule during the First World War. You will investigate the massive social, economic and political impact the war had on Russia which triggered the February Revolution and led to the tsar's abdication.
- Enquiry 3 looks at events between the February and October Revolutions. You will study the impact of Lenin's return to Russia, the weaknesses and failures of the Provisional Government, and the role played by the Petrograd Soviet. This enquiry culminates with the events of the Bolshevik revolution of October 1917.
- Enquiry 4 looks at how the Bolsheviks consolidated their power and the Russian Civil War. You will study the actions of the new government from their Decrees of 1917 to the reasons for victory in the Civil War.
- Enquiry 5 looks at economic changes brought in by the Bolsheviks. You will study why they introduced War Communism, what it was, and its disastrous impact on the people of Russia. You will investigate why the Bolsheviks responded by introducing the New Economic Policy and what opposition that faced. The enquiry finishes by weighing up Lenin's achievements before he died prematurely in 1924.

Key Individuals
Some of the key individuals studied on this course include:
- Tsar Nicholas II.
- Tsarina Alexandra.
- Rasputin.
- Vladimir Lenin.
- Joseph Stalin.
- Leon Trotsky.
- Alexander Kerensky.
- Pyotr Stolypin.

Key Events
Some of the key events you will study on this course include:
- Bloody Sunday, 1905.
- The Lena Goldfields Strike, 1912.
- The effect of the First World War on Russia.
- The February Revolution, 1917.
- The consolidation of Bolshevik control.
- The Russian Civil War.
- The New Economic Policy.

WHAT IS THIS BOOK ABOUT?

Assessment

Russia and the Soviet Union, 1905-24 forms part of paper 2 where you have a total of 1 hour and 30 minutes to complete. You should spend 45 minutes on this section of the paper. There will be 1 exam question, broken down into a, b and c, which will assess what you have learned on the Russia and the Soviet Union, 1905-24 course.

- Question a is worth 6 marks and will require you to describe two key features of one of two events given. You will need to identify two key features and support each with relevant factual detail.

- Question b is worth 8 marks. This question will require you to cross-reference two sources, explaining how one supports the evidence of the other, supported with evidence from both.

- Question c is worth 16 marks and requires you to explain how far you agree with an interpretation. In your explanation you must evaluate the interpretations, review alternative views, and use your own knowledge of the historical context as well as two sources to come to your conclusion.

Quizzes, amazing exam preparation tools and more at GCSEHistory.com

REVISION SUGGESTIONS

Revision! A dreaded word. Everyone knows it's coming, everyone knows how much it helps with your exam performance, and everyone struggles to get started! We know you want to do the best you can in your IGCSEs, but schools aren't always clear on the best way to revise. This can leave students wondering:

- ✓ How should I plan my revision time?
- ✓ How can I beat procrastination?
- ✓ What methods should I use? Flash cards? Re-reading my notes? Highlighting?

Luckily, you no longer need to guess at the answers. Education researchers have looked at all the available revision studies, and the jury is in. They've come up with some key pointers on the best ways to revise, as well as some thoughts on popular revision methods that aren't so helpful. The next few pages will help you understand what we know about the best revision methods.

How can I beat procrastination?

This is an age-old question, and it applies to adults as well! Have a look at our top three tips below.

◎ Reward yourself

When we think a task we have to do is going to be boring, hard or uncomfortable, we often put if off and do something more 'fun' instead. But we often don't really enjoy the 'fun' activity because we feel guilty about avoiding what we should be doing. Instead, get your work done and promise yourself a reward after you complete it. Whatever treat you choose will seem all the sweeter, and you'll feel proud for doing something you found difficult. Just do it!

◎ Just do it!

We tend to procrastinate when we think the task we have to do is going to be difficult or dull. The funny thing is, the most uncomfortable part is usually making ourselves sit down and start it in the first place. Once you begin, it's usually not nearly as bad as you anticipated.

◎ Pomodoro technique

The pomodoro technique helps you trick your brain by telling it you only have to focus for a short time. Set a timer for 20 minutes and focus that whole period on your revision. Turn off your phone, clear your desk, and work. At the end of the 20 minutes, you get to take a break for five. Then, do another 20 minutes. You'll usually find your rhythm and it becomes easier to carry on because it's only for a short, defined chunk of time.

Spaced practice

We tend to arrange our revision into big blocks. For example, you might tell yourself: "This week I'll do all my revision for the Cold War, then next week I'll do the Medicine Through Time unit."

Get our free app at GCSEHistory.com

REVISION SUGGESTIONS

This is called **massed practice**, because all revision for a single topic is done as one big mass.

But there's a better way! Try **spaced practice** instead. Instead of putting all revision sessions for one topic into a single block, space them out. See the example below for how it works.

This means planning ahead, rather than leaving revision to the last minute - but the evidence strongly suggests it's worth it. You'll remember much more from your revision if you use **spaced practice** rather than organising it into big blocks. Whichever method you choose, though, remember to reward yourself with breaks.

Spaced practice (more effective):

week 1	week 2	week 3	week 4
Topic 1	Topic 1	Topic 1	Topic 1
Topic 2	Topic 2	Topic 2	Topic 2
Topic 3	Topic 3	Topic 3	Topic 3
Topic 4	Topic 4	Topic 4	Topic 4

Massed practice (less effective)

week 1	week 2	week 3	week 4
Topic 1	Topic 2	Topic 3	Topic 4

Quizzes, amazing exam preparation tools and more at GCSEHistory.com

REVISION SUGGESTIONS

What methods should I use to revise?

Self-testing/flash cards

Self explanation/mind-mapping

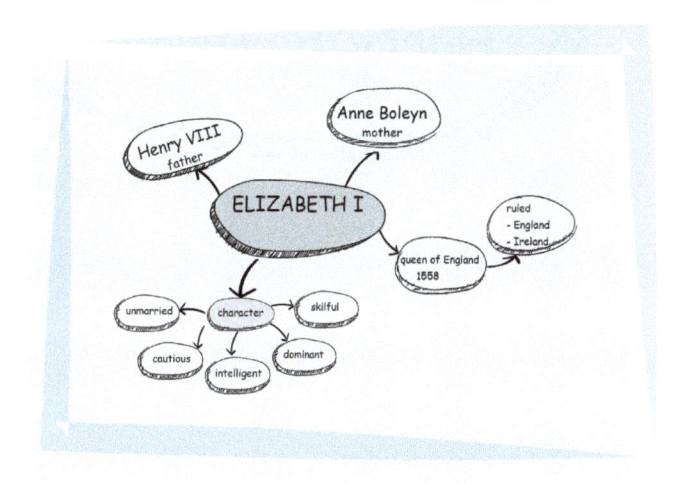

The research shows a clear winner for revision methods - **self-testing**. A good way to do this is with **flash cards**. Flash cards are really useful for helping you recall short – but important – pieces of information, like names and dates.

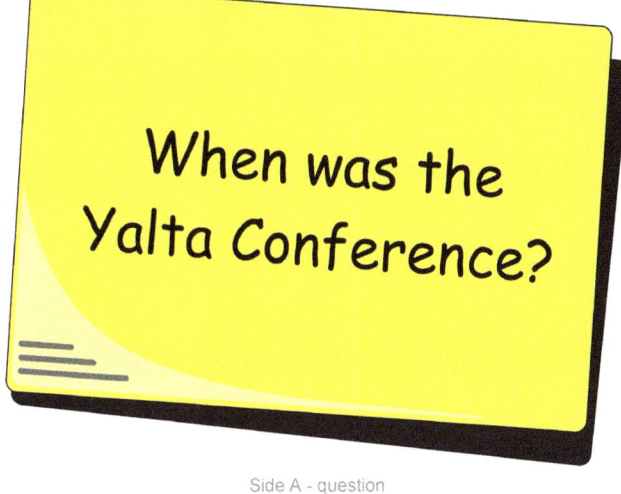

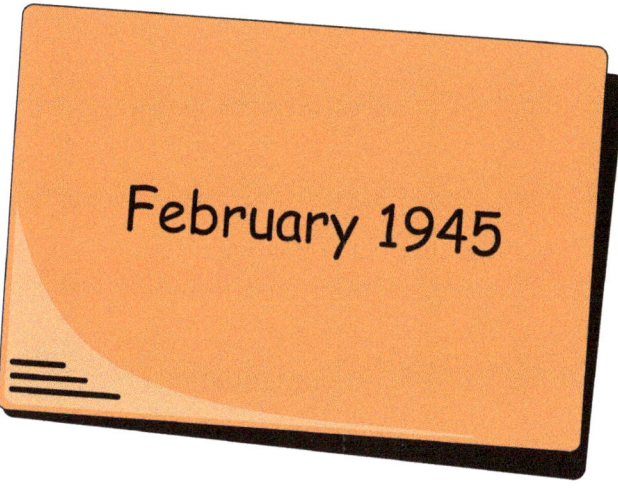

Side A - question

Side B - answer

Write questions on one side of the cards, and the answers on the back. This makes answering the questions and then testing yourself easy. Put all the cards you get right in a pile to one side, and only repeat the test with the ones you got wrong - this will force you to work on your weaker areas.

pile with right answers

pile with wrong answers

As this book has a quiz question structure itself, you can use it for this technique.

Another good revision method is **self-explanation**. This is where you explain how and why one piece of information from your course linked with another piece.

This can be done with **mind-maps**, where you draw the links and then write explanations for how they connect. For example, President Truman is connected with anti-communism because of the Truman Doctrine.

Get our free app at GCSEHistory.com

11

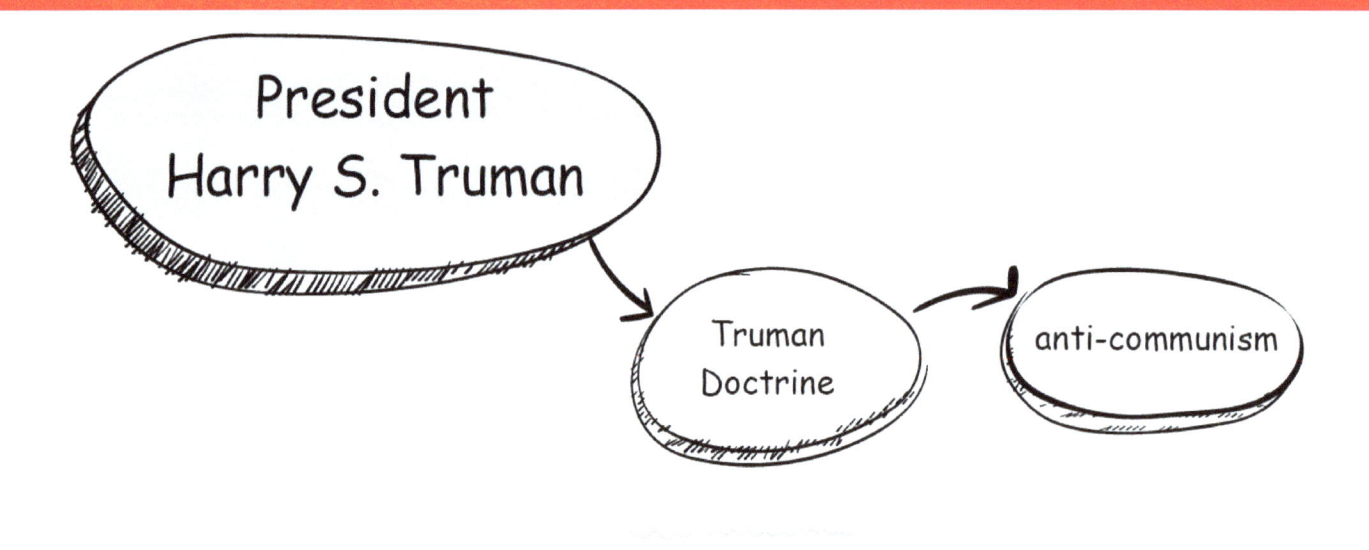

REVISION SUGGESTIONS

President Harry S. Truman → Truman Doctrine → anti-communism

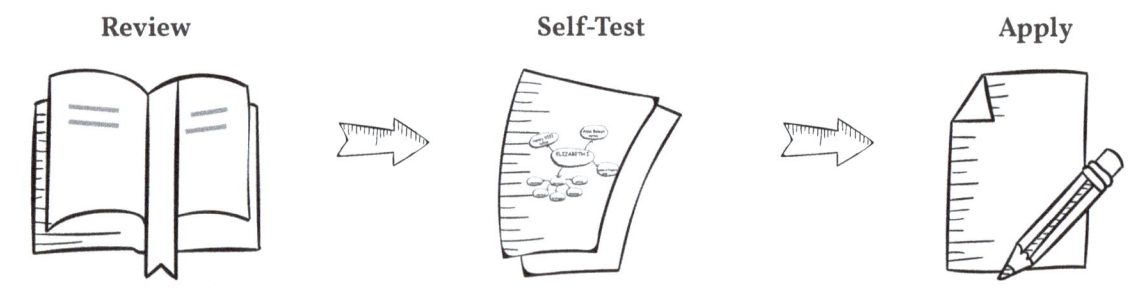

Review
Start by highlighting or re-reading to create your flashcards for self-testing.

Self-Test
Test yourself with flash cards. Make mind maps to explain the concepts.

Apply
Apply your knowledge on practice exam questions.

Which revision techniques should I be cautious about?

Highlighting and **re-reading** are not necessarily bad strategies - but the research does say they're less effective than flash cards and mind-maps.

Highlighting

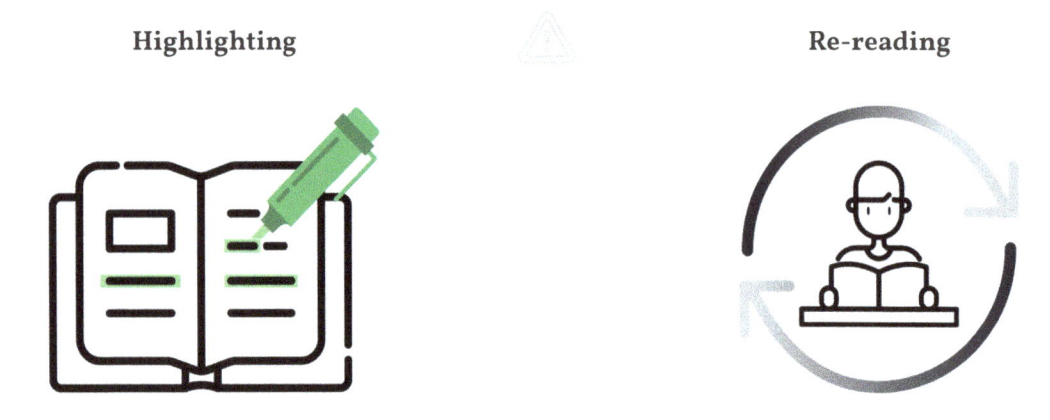

Re-reading

If you do use these methods, make sure they are **the first step to creating flash cards**. Really engage with the material as you go, rather than switching to autopilot.

Quizzes, amazing exam preparation tools and more at GCSEHistory.com

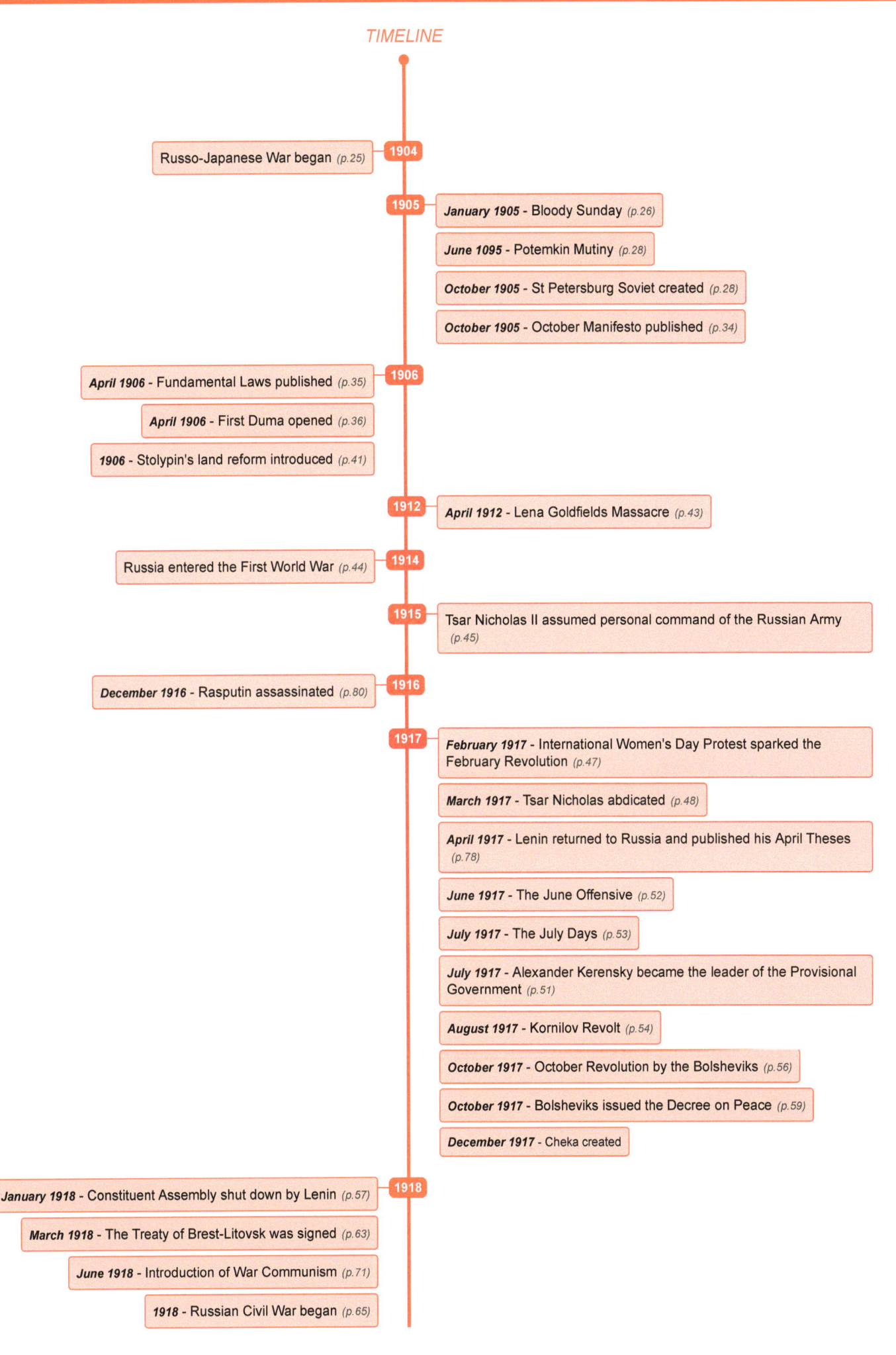

RUSSIA AND THE SOVIET UNION, 1905-24

TIMELINE

1904
- Russo-Japanese War began *(p.25)*

1905
- *January 1905* - Bloody Sunday *(p.26)*
- *June 1095* - Potemkin Mutiny *(p.28)*
- *October 1905* - St Petersburg Soviet created *(p.28)*
- *October 1905* - October Manifesto published *(p.34)*

1906
- *April 1906* - Fundamental Laws published *(p.35)*
- *April 1906* - First Duma opened *(p.36)*
- *1906* - Stolypin's land reform introduced *(p.41)*

1912
- *April 1912* - Lena Goldfields Massacre *(p.43)*

1914
- Russia entered the First World War *(p.44)*

1915
- Tsar Nicholas II assumed personal command of the Russian Army *(p.45)*

1916
- *December 1916* - Rasputin assassinated *(p.80)*

1917
- *February 1917* - International Women's Day Protest sparked the February Revolution *(p.47)*
- *March 1917* - Tsar Nicholas abdicated *(p.48)*
- *April 1917* - Lenin returned to Russia and published his April Theses *(p.78)*
- *June 1917* - The June Offensive *(p.52)*
- *July 1917* - The July Days *(p.53)*
- *July 1917* - Alexander Kerensky became the leader of the Provisional Government *(p.51)*
- *August 1917* - Kornilov Revolt *(p.54)*
- *October 1917* - October Revolution by the Bolsheviks *(p.56)*
- *October 1917* - Bolsheviks issued the Decree on Peace *(p.59)*
- *December 1917* - Cheka created

1918
- *January 1918* - Constituent Assembly shut down by Lenin *(p.57)*
- *March 1918* - The Treaty of Brest-Litovsk was signed *(p.63)*
- *June 1918* - Introduction of War Communism *(p.71)*
- *1918* - Russian Civil War began *(p.65)*

Get our free app at GCSEHistory.com

RUSSIA AND THE SOVIET UNION, 1905-24

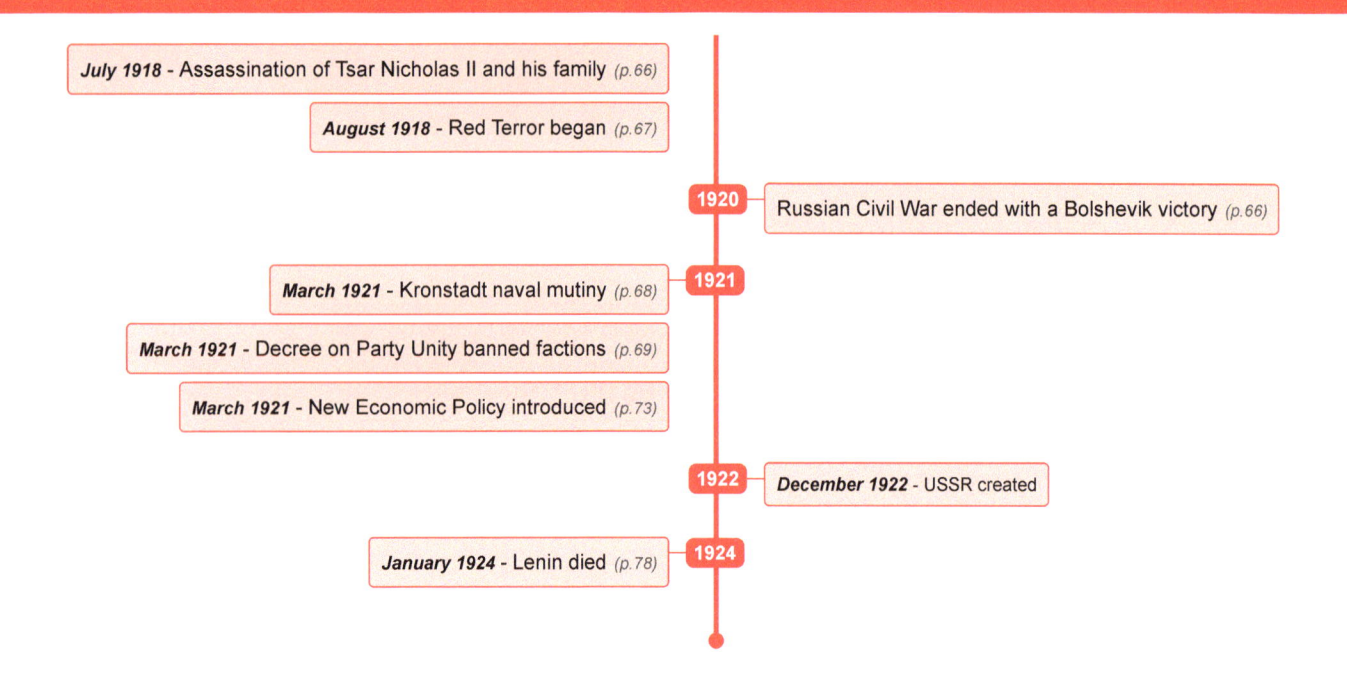

- *July 1918* - Assassination of Tsar Nicholas II and his family *(p.66)*
- *August 1918* - Red Terror began *(p.67)*

1920 — Russian Civil War ended with a Bolshevik victory *(p.66)*

1921
- *March 1921* - Kronstadt naval mutiny *(p.68)*
- *March 1921* - Decree on Party Unity banned factions *(p.69)*
- *March 1921* - New Economic Policy introduced *(p.73)*

1922 — *December 1922* - USSR created

1924 — *January 1924* - Lenin died *(p.78)*

INTRODUCTION TO RUSSIA IN THE EARLY 1900S

Churchill described Russia as, 'It is a riddle wrapped in a mystery inside an enigma.'

What was Russia like in the early 1900s?

In the early 1900s, Russia was an enormous empire which was economically and agriculturally backwards. It was ruled by an autocratic tsar *(p.19)*, who had absolute power, and suppressed all opposition.

How many ethnic groups lived in Russia in the early 1900s?

Russia had approximately 130 ethnic groups, who spoke over 100 different languages.

How big was Russia in the early 1900s?

In the early 1900s, Russia was an empire that stretched 6,000 miles, from the Baltic to the Pacific and from the Arctic down to central Asia.

Which countries did Russia border in the early 1900s?

Russia shared a border with the German Empire in Europe and China in the Far East, as well as Finland in the north and Afghanistan in the south.

What geographical problems did Russia have in the early 1900s?

The geographical size of Russia causes 6 main problems:

- Due to the size of the country, certain areas were difficult to control as they were far away from the tsarist capital, St Petersburg.
- Communication across the country was poor, leading some areas to be divided and detached.
- There were a lack of railways and useable roads.
- A large amount of land was unsuitable for farming.
- The peasants used backward and inefficient agricultural methods.
- With an increasing population, land was in short supply.

What type of government did Russia have in the early 1900s?

There were 6 key features of tsarist government:

- The tsars were emperors who ruled with absolute power. Their power was justified by the belief that they possessed the divine right to rule.
- There was an Imperial Council who advised the tsar *(p.19)*, whose members came from the nobility. The tsar appointed or dismissed its members, therefore the nobles were often corrupt and more interested in securing their position in the Imperial Council than providing balanced advice.
- There was a Committee of Ministers who ran 13 different departments (increased to 14 in 1900). The ministers were appointed by the tsar *(p.19)* and their decisions needed his approval.
- There was a massive bureaucracy to run such a huge country. It was slow and often corrupt.
- Russia was divided into 117 different provinces which were run by the nobles. The governors of the provinces were responsible for enforcing the tsar's *(p.19)* laws, which they could do with some degree of independence.
- It relied on the Imperial Army, the Russian Orthodox Church and the police to keep control.

How developed was industry in Russia in the early 1900s?

There were 6 main issues with Russia's level of industrialisation:

- It had a low-level of industry but it was growing quickly. By 1914, Russia was the world's 4th largest producer of coal, pig iron and steel.

- Its banking system was backwards and could not support the investment needed to modernise the country.
- It lacked workers for new industries as many peasants were tied to their villages because of the debts they owed to their landlords.
- There was extreme poverty in Russia, therefore there was little demand for manufactured goods making investment for modernisation very difficult.
- The level of industrialisation was uneven across the empire. The industrial cities tended to be in the western parts of Russia.
- It lacked a developed transport network. There were few paved roads and although railways were developing, they were inadequate for helping Russia modernise.

What was farming like in Russia in the early 1900s?

There were 6 main issues with Russian agriculture:

- Agriculture was backward with little use of modern technology. Most peasants were subsistence farmers who mainly used traditional methods of farming because they had little to no education or opportunity to modernise.
- The peasants were emancipated in 1861, which meant they were free from serfdom. In practice, serfdom was replaced with debt slavery, forcing the peasants to take on loans in order to buy back their land.
- The Russian countryside experienced frequent famines and crop failures, leading to food shortages and starvation.
- The government failed to successfully deal with famines through a combination of the tsar's *(p.19)* indifference to suffering, poor infrastructure, local corruption and the nobles' mismanagement of the land.
- Most peasants were illiterate, poorly informed and resistant to change.
- The village commune, or mir, controlled how the peasants farmed and on which land they farmed. The mir allocated small strips of land to village peasants which was very often an ineffective and unproductive way to farm.

What were conditions like in Russia in the early 1900s?

By the 1900s, the living and working conditions in Russian town were terrible for 3 main reasons:

- Workers usually shared filthy rooms in block-style buildings.
- There could be up to 10 people sharing a room in these buildings, including men, women and children.
- Although working days were officially limited to 11 hours per day, the average working day was 15-16 hours.

What were the main religions of Russia in the early 1900s?

In the early 1900s, the 3 main religions were:

- Russian Orthodox, a form of Christianity, and the official state religion of Russia.
- Judaism. There were about 5 million Jews.
- Islam. There were about 23 million Muslims.

What role did the Church play in Russia in the early 1900s?

The Russian Orthodox Church played a very important role in Russia in 4 main ways:

- It taught the Russian people to love and obey the tsar *(p.19)* as the 'Little Father'.
- It underpinned the tsarist government as many Church leaders were from the aristocratic class of Russia's rulers who owned vast country estates.
- It was very conservative in nature and used its influence to block any change in Russia that might upset its position in society.
- It played a large role in education by teaching children to show loyalty to the tsar *(p.19)*, his officials, and the Church.

What different social classes existed in Russia in the early 1900s?

There were 7 different groups that made up Russian society by the late 1800s:

- The aristocrats made up about 1% of the population but owned 25% of the land.

- The clergy made up 0.5% of the population.
- The middle class of small bankers, merchants and professionals made up about 0.5% of the population.
- There was a class called 'urbanities' which consisted of small tradesmen, shopkeepers, white collar workers and artisans that made up 11% of the population.
- Cossacks made up about 2.3% of the population.
- The peasants made up about 80% of the population, an overwhelming majority, and were exceptionally poor and illiterate.
- About 8% was made up of other groups.

What different nationalities made up Russia in the early 1900s?

In the early 1900s, Russia was made up of several different nationalities. The 5 main ones were:
- Slavs (including Belarusians, Russians, and Ukrainians).
- Poles.
- Asians.
- Germans.
- Latvians, Estonians and Lithuanians.

> **DID YOU KNOW?**
>
> **3 facts about Russia:**
> - Great Britain could almost fit 100 times into the Russian Empire.
> - The temperature could range from -60 degrees centigrade in the winter and to 40 degrees centigrade in the summer.
> - Northern Siberia may only be frost-free for 2 months a year.

THE RUSSIAN CALENDAR
Julius Caesar brought in the Julian calendar in 45BC.

What happened to the Russian calendar?

Russia has used two different calendars in the last 100 years: the Julian calendar and the Gregorian calendar.

When did the calendar change in Russia?

The old-style Julian calendar was replaced by the Gregorian calendar in January 1918.

What difference did the change to the Russian calendar make?

There were 2 main changes:
- The change from the Julian to the Gregorian calendar meant the loss of 13 days.
- Events that occurred before January 1918 have two dates. For example, the Bolshevik (p.32) Revolution occurred on 7th November, 1918 under the Gregorian calendar and on 25th October under the old Julian calendar.

> **DID YOU KNOW?**
>
> **The Bolsheviks brought in the change from the old style Julian calendar to the new Gregorian calendar after the October Revolution.**
>
> Most of western Europe had adopted the Gregorian calendar by the mid-1700s.

TSARIST RULE

Tsar Nicholas II stated in 1905, 'I shall never, under any circumstances, agree to a representative form of government because I consider it harmful to the people whom God has entrusted to my care.'

Who were the tsars?

The tsars were the kings or emperors who ruled Russia. They were autocrats which meant they had absolute power and could make any decision they liked. The position of the tsar was passed down the royal family from father to son.

Who helped the tsars govern Russia?

The tsars relied on the 5 key groups or organisations to rule Russia:

- ☑ Aristocratic ministers gave the tsars advice.
- ☑ The Russian Orthodox Church would support the tsars.
- ☑ The secret police, called the Okhrana, would crush any opposition.
- ☑ The army and navy swore an oath of loyalty to the tsar. The army could be used to crush any opposition.
- ☑ The zemstvos, or locally elected assemblies, set up to administer local affairs which were controlled by aristocrats.

How did the tsars control the countryside?

There were 4 key ways in which the tsars controlled the peasants:

- ☑ The peasants were freed in 1861 and were no longer serfs. However, they were in debt to the landowners because of this.
- ☑ A mir, or village commune, controlled the peasants.
- ☑ Law and order in the countryside was in the hands of the nobles.
- ☑ The zemstvos, or locally elected assemblies, were also controlled by the nobles.

How did the tsars select their ministers?

The tsars selected their ministers from 2 main groups:

- ☑ The aristocracy who were the people in the highest social class in Russia - they had land, money and power.
- ☑ The most senior officials in the Russian Orthodox Church.

What were the tsars responsible for?

The tsar was in charge of everything in the country. He had authority over the Church, all laws, taxation, the army and the navy.

Get our free app at GCSEHistory.com

> **DID YOU KNOW?**
>
> **The tsars of Russia believed in their divine right to rule.**
> In 2000, Tsar Nicholas II, Tsarina Alexandra and their children were canonised by the Russian Orthodox Church; they were made saints.

TSAR NICHOLAS II

Tsar Nicholas was ill-equipped to rule Russia.

Who was Tsar Nicholas II?

Tsar Nicholas II was the last tsar *(p. 19)* of Russia. He was a part of the Romanov royal family that had ruled the nation since 1613.

When did Tsar Nicholas II rule Russia?

Tsar Nicholas II ruled Russia from 1894 to 1917.

How did Tsar Nicholas II rule Russia?

Nicholas II was an autocrat who had absolute power to do what he wanted.

Who helped Tsar Nicholas II to rule Russia?

Nicholas II relied on the following 4 institutions or organisations to rule Russia:

- The aristocracy.
- The Okhrana (secret police).
- The army.
- The Russian Orthodox Church.

What was Tsar Nicholas II like?

Nicholas II's rule of Russia was problematic for 5 main reasons:

- He had not been prepared for what the role would entail.
- He was a poor decision-maker and often procrastinated when faced with difficult decisions.
- His own lack of ability meant he was often jealous of his ministers. This created distrust and tension.
- He was very conservative by nature and determined to uphold his autocratic rule at all costs.
- His marriage to Alexandra Feodorovna, a German princess, led to problems as she became unpopular during the First World War. She made grave errors of judgement as the regent of Russia, a role she held while Nicholas commanded troops at the front.

What problems did Tsar Nicholas II face as the leader of Russia?

There were 5 main problems that Nicholas II faced as the ruler of Russia:

- Ensuring Russia was ruled effectively and efficiently.
- Modernising agriculture to become more productive, ensuring there were food surpluses to sell abroad. This gained money that was invested in the economy.

- ✓ Modernising Russian industry so that it could compete with Britain, Germany and the USA, and remain a great power.
- ✓ Reducing social and political unrest as different groups demanded reform.
- ✓ Ensuring Russian security in Europe and Asia as the international situation deteriorated, particularly with Japan, Germany and the Austro-Hungarian Empire.

What was Tsar Nicholas II's policy of Russification?

Russification (p.42) was a policy implemented by the tsars to force non-Russian minorities to partake in Russian culture and language. Due to this policy, discrimination against non-Russians became more open. This led to an increase in minority-based opposition to the tsars.

How did Tsar Nicholas II deal with opposition to his rule?

Tsar Nicholas II dealt with opposition to his rule in 5 key ways:

- ✓ He used the Okhrana, or secret police, to keep watch on suspected revolutionaries. Undercover agents would spy on groups.
- ✓ Revolutionaries and terrorists were prosecuted in court and either executed or exiled. Many executions were public to create fear.
- ✓ Government censorship of books and newspapers stopped the spread of any radical ideas that could undermine the tsarist government.
- ✓ When there were uprisings, such as Bloody Sunday in 1905, he used the army to crush the protesters.
- ✓ He brought in some reforms in an attempt to make some concessions to discontented groups, such as the reforms in his October Manifesto (p.34) in 1905.

Why was Tsar Nicholas II important?

There were 6 key events during Nicholas II's reign:

- ✓ His government was not viewed favourably because it failed to improve the lives of ordinary citizens and failed to reform.
- ✓ Russia was humiliated when it was defeated in the Russo-Japanese War (p.25), 1904-05.
- ✓ Russia did very badly during the First World War and its people suffered as a result.
- ✓ There were several revolutions against his rule; one in 1905 and one in February 1917.
- ✓ He was forced to abdicate in March 1917.
- ✓ He was eventually executed by the Bolsheviks (p.32) during the Russian Civil War (p.65).

How successful was Tsar Nicholas II in ruling Russia?

Tsar Nicholas II's government had 4 main successes:

- ✓ He managed to stay in power after the 1905 Revolution (until the February 1917 Revolution) and maintain a predominantly autocratic government.
- ✓ Some political reforms were brought in after the 1905 Revolution including the creation of the State Duma (p.36) (a parliament), voting rights and legalisation of political parties.
- ✓ Some economic reforms were introduced by Pyotr Stolypin to improve the working conditions of industrial workers.
- ✓ There was some economic development in terms of greater industrialisation. For example, there was a 50% increase in iron and steel production before the First World War.

How did Tsar Nicholas II fail?

Tsar Nicholas II's government failed in 5 key ways:

- ✓ He was a poor military leader and failed to defend Russia from her enemies. Russia was defeated in the Russo-Japanese War (p.25) and was doing incredibly badly in the First World War when he was forced to abdicate.

- ✅ He failed to bring in real political reforms to make Russia more democratic and this failure created even more political opposition.
- ✅ He failed to improve agriculture so there wasn't enough food for the growing population.
- ✅ He was a poor political leader, weak at ruling the country, who made poor decisions.
- ✅ Living and working conditions for workers and peasants did not improve; their wages stayed low while the cost of living rose.

When did Tsar Nicholas II die?
Nicholas II died on 17th July, 1918.

How did Tsar Nicholas II die?
The Bolsheviks *(p.32)* executed Tsar Nicholas II and his family by firing squad. Their bodies were then disposed of down a well.

> **DID YOU KNOW?**
>
> **Tsar Nicholas II wrote in his diary:**
> 'What is going to happen to me and all of Russia? I am not prepared to be a Tsar. I never wanted to become one. I know nothing of the business of ruling.'

TSARIST POLICE STATE
The tsarist form of government relied on the suppression of the police, army and church to rule.

What was the tsarist police state?
The tsarist police state was how the tsars, like Nicholas II, ruled Russia. They used the police, the law, the courts, and censorship to control the people.

What was the role of censorship in the tsarist police state?
The tsarist government banned radical ideas from being printed. All books and newspapers were censored.

What was the Okhrana's role in the tsarist police state?
The Okhrana were the state secret police. They spied on people suspected of being revolutionaries or opposed to the regime.

How were people who opposed the tsar punished in the tsarist police state?
People who were accused of opposing the tsarist regime were put in prison, exiled to Siberia, or executed.

> **DID YOU KNOW?**
>
> **The Cossacks were mounted soldiers that the tsars relied upon for suppressing rebellions.**
>
> The Cossacks played an important role in crushing the 1905 Revolution but turned against the tsar in the February 1917 Revolution.

DISCONTENT

Most social classes in Russia were discontented.

What were the reasons for discontent in Russia in 1905?

There were a range of political, economic, social, and military problems that were causing discontent and unhappiness among different social classes in tsarist Russia by 1905.

What caused discontent in tsarist Russia in 1905?

There were 6 key reasons for discontent in Russia in 1905:

- The peasants were exceptionally poor, wanted more land and wanted taxes to be reduced.
- Industrial workers were angry about their working and living conditions, low pay and the high unemployment rates.
- Middle class people were frustrated they had no say in how the country was run because it was an autocracy. They wanted more freedom, but were afraid of revolution.
- Non-Russians did not want to be ruled by Russians and wanted their independence.
- There were radical groups that wanted to overthrow the tsar *(p.19)* and give power to the workers or peasants.
- Many people hated the police and secret police because they curtailed their freedom.

What caused discontent in the countryside in Russia 1905?

The peasants were unhappy because they were suffering in 4 main ways:

- The peasants were exceptionally poor, most were subsistence farmers and they needed more land.
- There were many famines which affected the Russian Empire in the 1890s and 1901. Thousands of people died.
- The tsar *(p.19)* and his government did not deal very well with the famines and the peasants were angry.
- Many peasants were in debt. From 1861 they were no longer owned by the landowners but had to pay for their freedom.

What caused discontent in the middle classes in Russia in 1905?

There were 4 main reasons the middle class was unhappy:

- Many wanted political reforms such as the freedom of speech or the right to vote which had been granted in other European countries.
- Many wanted to remove the tsar *(p.19)* and have a written constitution which would give everyone equal rights.
- Many were terrified of the revolutionary political groups that had developed in Russia as the middle class would lose out if a revolution occurred.
- They were frustrated with Tsar Nicholas II's *(p.20)* unwillingness to implement political reform.

What caused discontent in the industrial workers in tsarist Russia?

There were 4 main reasons why the industrial workers were unhappy:

- Their working conditions were awful and dangerous.
- Their pay was very poor.
- Their living conditions were terrible as their pay was so low they could not afford anywhere better to live and often lived in overcrowded conditions.
- Workers suffered from illnesses and often became alcoholics as a result of their living conditions.

Why were non-Russians unhappy in tsarist Russia?

There were 3 key reasons why non-Russians were unhappy:

- ✅ The Russian Empire contained some 19 different nationalities in the areas conquered by the tsars over the years. Those areas wanted their independence.
- ✅ Russia forced 'Russification *(p.42)*' on the non-Russian areas.
- ✅ Russian people got preferential treatment e.g. Russians were given jobs in the local government in preference to the local people.

How did discontent relate to political opposition in tsarist Russia?

There were 3 main issues with political opposition:

- ✅ Political parties were illegal so people could not express their political views.
- ✅ Despite being illegal, political groups that opposed the tsarist regime were set up. For example, groups included the Populists, Social Democrats, Social Revolutionaries, the Mensheviks and the Bolsheviks *(p.32)*.
- ✅ Some groups like the Social Revolutionaries, Social Democrats, the Mensheviks and the Bolsheviks *(p.32)* wanted to completely remove the tsarist regime through revolution.

> **DID YOU KNOW?**
>
> Tsar Alexander II claimed that 'it is not difficult to rule Russia, but it is useless.'

POLITICAL OPPOSITION TO THE TSAR

Political opposition to the tsarist form of government had been growing since the mid-1800s.

What political opposition was there to Tsar Nicholas II?

Opposition to Tsar Nicholas II was growing because he would not allow political reform and did not improve living conditions.

When was there political opposition to Tsar Nicholas II?

Opposition to the tsarist regime was growing throughout the 1800s and early 1900s, although political parties were illegal until October 1905.

Why was there political opposition to Tsar Nicholas II?

Political opposition to Nicholas II was growing because of 3 key reasons:

- ✅ Some groups wanted to limit the power of Nicholas II.
- ✅ Some wanted radical change and to completely remove Nicholas II from power.
- ✅ Most groups wanted to see reforms brought in to improve the social, economic, and political conditions in Russia.

Who was the political opposition to Tsar Nicholas II?

There were several different groups that opposed Nicholas II such as the Liberals (split into the Kadets and the Octobrists), the Socialist Revolutionary Party *(p.30)*, and the Social Democratic Party *(p.32)*.

Why did Tsar Nicholas II face opposition from the Social Democratic Party?

The Social Democratic Party *(p.32)* was set up in 1898 and:

- ✅ Believed in communism and the ideas of Karl Marx.
- ✅ Wanted a revolution to get rid of Nicholas II and the tsarist government.

- Believed in giving power to the workers.
- They wanted to establish a communist state.
- In 1903 they split into the moderate Mensheviks and the more revolutionary Bolsheviks. *(p.32)*

Why did Tsar Nicholas II face opposition from Socialist Revolutionary Party?

The Socialist Revolutionary Party *(p.30)* wanted to end the tsarist regime:

- Some believed in using terrorism to achieve this and assassinated Tsar *(p.19)* Alexander II in 1881. They were responsible for around 2,000 assassinations between 1901 and 1905.
- Others believed in working with other political groups to improve working and living conditions.

Why did Tsar Nicholas II face opposition from the Liberals?

Some groups such as the Kadets wanted a constitutional government in which the tsar *(p.19)* remained as the head of state. However, his power was to be limited by a constitution, and there would be a democratically elected government.

DID YOU KNOW?

Political discontent had been increasing for many years when Nicholas became the tsar.

Nicholas II own grandfather, Tsar Alexander II, was assassinated in 1881 and there were several attempts to assassinate his father, Tsar Alexander III.

THE RUSSO-JAPANESE WAR, 1904-05

The Russo-Japanese War was a national humiliation for Russia.

What was the Russo-Japanese War?

The Russo-Japanese War was a conflict between the Russian Empire, ruled by Tsar Nicholas II *(p.20)*, and Imperial Japan under Emperor Meiji.

When was the Russo-Japanese War?

The Russo-Japanese War began on 8th February, 1904, and ended on 5th September (23rd August, Old Style), 1905.

Why did the Russo-Japanese War happen?

There were 5 key causes of the Russo-Japanese War:

- Russia wanted to expand its territory in China in an area called Manchuria. This brought Russia into conflict with Japan, which was trying to do the same.
- Tsar Nicholas II *(p.20)* wanted a 'short, swift victorious' war to reduce opposition at home which was growing due to deteriorating conditions.
- Russia needed ports that could be used all year as its existing ports froze over in winter.
- The Russians did not believe Japan, as an Asian nation, would be able to beat them as they considered them inferior.
- Russia was considering expanding the Trans-Siberian Railway into Manchuria. The Japanese saw that as a threat to their position in Korea.

What happened during the Russo-Japanese War?

There were 6 key events of the war:

- ☑ In January 1904, Port Arthur, a Russian naval base, was attacked by the Japanese.
- ☑ In February 1905, Russia was defeated in the Battle of Mukden and surrendered it to Japan.
- ☑ In May 1905, at the Battle of Tsushima, the Russian Baltic fleet was defeated by the Japanese navy.
- ☑ In August 1905, the Japanese won a major land battle in the Battle of Liaoyang despite having a smaller force.
- ☑ In January 1905, Port Arthur surrendered to the Japanese.
- ☑ In September 1905, both sides formally ended the war when they signed the Treaty of Portsmouth.

What was the significance of the Russo-Japanese War for Russia?

Russia's defeat in the Russo-Japanese War was significant for 4 reasons:

- ☑ Tsar Nicholas II *(p.20)* was blamed for the humiliation of being defeated by Japan, which had been considered a lesser power.
- ☑ The military defeats in the war helped cause the mutiny on the Battleship Potemkin in June 1905.
- ☑ Fighting the war put even more strain on the government's resources and diverted much-needed grain and fuel away from the people, creating even more discontent.
- ☑ It was a key trigger of the 1905 Revolution and Bloody Sunday incident.

DID YOU KNOW?

Japan's navy included many British-built battleships.

BLOODY SUNDAY, 1905

Bloody Sunday in 1905 seriously undermined the authority of Tsar Nicholas II.

What was Bloody Sunday?

Bloody Sunday is the name of a massacre that happened in St Petersburg. Around 200 people were killed.

When was Bloody Sunday?

Bloody Sunday happened on Sunday, 22nd January, 1905 (9th January, Old Style).

Why did Bloody Sunday happen in 1905?

There were 5 key reasons for the protest:

- ☑ The protesters wanted a constitution which would protect the rights of the people.
- ☑ They marched to present a petition to Tsar Nicholas II *(p.20)* complaining about working conditions.
- ☑ They wanted to be able to set up trade unions to protect the rights of workers.
- ☑ They wanted to only work eight hours a day.
- ☑ They wanted a minimum wage of one rouble per day.

What happened during Bloody Sunday?

The 5 key events of Bloody Sunday were:

- A large group of protesters, made up of workers and their families, gathered in St Petersburg led by Father Gapon.
- Soldiers blocked the protesters' route to the tsar's *(p.19)* palace.
- Warning shots were fired.
- Mounted Cossacks attacked the protesters and then the soldiers fired at the crowd.
- 200 people died and 800 were wounded.

What was the importance of Bloody Sunday in Russia?

The Bloody Sunday massacre encouraged 4 key further protests:

- The Potemkin mutiny in June 1905.
- Peasant riots across Russia between 1905 and 1907.
- Strikes across Russia by workers.
- The creation of soviets, or workers' councils.

Why did Tsar Nicholas II survive the consequences of Bloody Sunday?

There are 6 key reasons Nicholas II survived Bloody Sunday:

- The army stayed loyal to him and crushed the demonstration.
- He issued the October Manifesto *(p.34)* which won over the middle class and liberals as it appeared to give them power through the setting up of a State Duma *(p.36)*, or parliament.
- Pyotr Stolypin, as Minister of the Interior and then the Prime Minister, used the army and police to crush all political opposition.
- Any person suspected of being a revolutionary was arrested and imprisoned.
- Newspapers and trade unions were closed.
- The opposition was split between different groups such as workers, sailors, peasants and minority nationalities that wanted different things.

DID YOU KNOW?

There was much criticism of Tsar Nicholas II's suppression of the demonstrators.
America, Britain and France all condemned his actions.

THE 1905 REVOLUTION

Tsar Nicholas II survived the upheaval of the 1905 Revolution by satisfying some of the key discontented groups.

What was the Russian Revolution of 1905?

Russia faced massive social and political unrest during the Revolution of 1905. Some of this was directed at the government.

When was the Russian Revolution of 1905?

The Russian Revolution of 1905 started on 22nd January that year. Unrest lasted until 1907.

What caused the Russian Revolution of 1905?

There were 5 causes of the 1905 revolution:

- ☑ One long-term cause was discontent amongst the peasants because they were heavily taxed, incredibly poor, and suffered from famines and hunger on a regular basis.
- ☑ Another long-term cause was discontent among industrial workers because they had terrible working and living conditions and very low pay. Unemployment was rising in the early 1900s.
- ☑ A third long-term cause was the growth in political opposition to Nicholas II from different groups such as the country's different nationalities and political organisations, such as the Social Revolutionaries.
- ☑ An immediate cause was Russia's defeat in the Russo-Japanese War *(p.25)* of 1904-05. Tsar Nicholas II *(p.20)* was blamed for the defeat and lost support as a result.
- ☑ A major trigger cause was Bloody Sunday. On 22nd January, unarmed civilians led by Father Gapon were shot by tsarist soldiers in St Petersburg.

What events occurred during the 1905 Russian Revolution?

There were 7 key events during the 1905 revolution:

- ☑ There was a mutiny by sailors on the navy battleship Potemkin over poor quality food. This resulted in the deaths of some officers and sailors on 14th June, 1905.
- ☑ The Potemkin sailed to the port of Odessa where strikers and protesters showed their support for the sailors. There were riots, which Nicholas II ordered the army to stop. 1,000 people were shot dead.
- ☑ There were riots across Russia by peasants between 1905 and 1907. They burned their landlords' homes and created communes to share the land.
- ☑ Industrial workers announced a general strike between 20th September and 2nd October, 1905.
- ☑ The workers organised into soviets, or worker councils, in St Petersburg and Moscow by October 1905. These were elected councils which demanded better conditions. Leon Trotsky became the chairman of the St Petersburg Soviet.
- ☑ The government issued the October Manifesto *(p.34)* on 17th October. This granted civil rights, a parliament called a Duma *(p.36)*, and promised new laws would be discussed.
- ☑ Unrest continued across the country which was quashed by the army. The most notable was the crushing of the Moscow Soviet uprising led by Social Democrats in December 1905, which resulted in over 1,000 people being killed.

What was the government's response to the 1905 Russian Revolution?

Nicholas II's government took 4 key actions:

- ☑ They crushed many of the protests. For example, the army shot the protesters in Odessa and in Moscow in December 1905, when the Moscow Soviet tried to organise an uprising.
- ☑ They closed down the soviets. For example, the St Petersburg Soviet was shut down in December 1905.
- ☑ The tsar *(p.19)* issued the October Manifesto *(p.34)* on 17th October, which granted civil rights, a parliament called a Duma *(p.36)*, and promised new laws would be discussed by the new parliament.
- ☑ There was a harsh and violent crackdown on any opposition. There were arrests with many people exiled or put to death - more than 1000 people were executed between 1906 and 1907.

What was the outcome of the Russian Revolution of 1905?

There were 4 main results of the Revolution of 1905.

- ☑ Nicholas II and his government survived.
- ☑ The strikers and the revolutionaries were defeated.
- ☑ The October Manifesto *(p.34)* was published.
- ☑ A state Duma *(p.36)* was created.

Why did Nicholas II survive the 1905 Russian Revolution?

There were 3 key reasons Nicholas II survived the 1905 Revolution:

- The military, on the whole, still supported Nicholas II and crushed the uprisings.
- He made concessions which pleased the liberals and the middle classes; these changes were detailed in the October Manifesto *(p.34)*.
- The opposition was split between different groups that wanted different things.

> **DID YOU KNOW?**
>
> The 1925 film 'Battleship Potemkin', directed by Sergei Eisenstein, tells the story of the 1905 mutiny which contributed to the revolution. It has often been lauded as one of the greatest films of all time.

THE OCTOBRIST PARTY

The Octobrists were named after the October Manifesto which they supported.

Who were the Octobrists?

The Octobrist Party was a Russian political party with socially conservative, but constitutionally liberal views. It was created in November 1905.

When was the Octobrist Party set up?

The Octobrist Party existed from 1905 to 1917, when they were made illegal by the Bolshevik *(p.32)* Party.

Why was the Octobrist Party set up?

The Octobrist Party was set up after Tsar Nicholas II *(p.20)* issued his October Manifesto *(p.34)* to support the implementation of the changes the October Manifesto.

What were the views of the Octobrist Party?

The Octobrists had 2 key views:

- They believed in a limited constitutional monarchy in which the State Duma *(p.36)* passed laws but the tsar *(p.19)* kept his authority.
- They initially supported Stolypin's economic policies but became more critical because of his repressive policies.

What was the role of the Octobrist Party in the Duma?

The Octobrists played 4 main roles in the State Dumas:

- The Octobrists became the largest group in the third Duma *(p.38)* because Stolypin changed the voting laws in 1907.
- They supported Russia's entry into the First World War in 1914.
- They joined the Progressive Bloc in 1915 with the Kadets, or Constitutional Democratic Party *(p.31)*, which wanted more representative leadership and reform.
- They held several positions in the government during the First World War and the Dual Power of the Provisional Government *(p.50)* and the Petrograd Soviet *(p.49)* in 1917.

DID YOU KNOW?

The Octobrists were led by Alexander Guchkov.
He would later become minister of war in the Provisional Government.

THE SOCIALIST REVOLUTIONARY PARTY

The Socialist Revolutionaries were prepared to use violence to achieve their aims.

What was the Socialist Revolutionary Party?

The Socialist Revolutionary Party was a Russian political party that wanted to end the tsarist regime - some of of its members were happy to use violence.

When was the Socialist Revolutionary Party important?

The Socialist Revolutionary Party was created in 1902 and made illegal by the Bolsheviks *(p.32)* in 1917.

What did the Socialist Revolutionary Party believe?

The Socialist Revolutionary Party believed in land reform, so there would be no private ownership of land. Instead, it would be held by the communes.

What tactics did the Socialist Revolutionary Party use?

The Socialist Revolutionary Party often committed political assassinations and used terrorist tactics.

DID YOU KNOW?

The Social Revolutionaries committed many assassinations.
- ✔ They committed approximately 2,000 assassinations before the 1905 Revolution.
- ✔ They were infiltrated by the Okhrana who reported on their activities.
- ✔ One of the most the famous assassination of the Social Revolutionaries was of Stolypin.

THE TRUDOVIK PARTY

Trudovik means 'labour' and they were a political party representing peasant farmers.

What was the Trudovik Party?

The Trudovik Party was a Russian political party created in 1906 when the Socialist Revolutionary Party *(p.30)* refused to take part in the first Duma *(p.36)*.

When was the Trudovik Party created?

The Trudovik Party was created in 1906 and was very important during the first and second Dumas of Russia because they won many seats. They were made illegal by the Bolsheviks *(p.32)* in 1917.

Why was the Trudovik Party created?

Some members of the Socialist Revolutionary Party *(p.30)* created a new party, the Trudoviks, because they opposed the party's decision to not participate in the first Duma *(p.36)*.

What were the views of the Trudovik Party?

The Trudovik Party's main belief was in land reform. It thought all land ownership should be in the hands of the peasants. They supported the Provisional Government *(p.50)*.

DID YOU KNOW?

Alexander Kerensky was a member of the Trudovik Party.

THE KADETS

The Constitutional Democratic Party or Kadets were liberals mainly supported by the middle and upper classes.

Who were the Kadets?

The Kadets, or Constitutional Democratic Party, was a Russian political party established in 1906 that had liberal beliefs.

When was the Kadet Party important?

The Kadets, or Constitutional Democratic Party, was created in 1906 and made illegal by the Bolsheviks *(p.32)* in 1917. They were very important in the first Duma *(p.36)* as they were the largest party.

What did the Kadet Party believe?

The Kadets had 3 main beliefs:

- ✅ They wanted a constitutional monarchy similar to Britain.
- ✅ Universal, free and equal suffrage (voting rights).
- ✅ Land reform to favour the peasants but which compensated the landlords.

DID YOU KNOW?

The Kadets leader was Pavel Milyukov and Prince Lvov was one of their leading members.

THE SOCIAL DEMOCRATIC PARTY

The Social Democratic Party believed in communism.

Who were the Social Democratic Party?
The Russian Social Democratic Party was created in 1898 and followed Karl Marx's ideas about communist revolution.

When was the Social Democratic Party important?
The Social Democratic Party was important from its creation, in 1898, until it split into 2 separate parties in 1903.

What did the Social Democratic Party believe?
The Social Democratic Party believed in communism and the need for a revolution in Russia to overthrow the tsarist regime.

Why did the Social Democratic Party split?
The Social Democratic Party split in 1903 because there was a disagreement about how to achieve a communist revolution:
- ☑ The Mensheviks believed the revolution would only happen after Russia industrialised and created a large working class. This would take a long time.
- ☑ The Bolsheviks *(p.32)* believed that the revolution in Russia could happen more quickly if a small group of dedicated revolutionaries led the revolution and set up a dictatorship of the proletariat on behalf of the workers.

> **DID YOU KNOW?**
>
> Communism is a political ideology developed by Karl Marx.

THE BOLSHEVIK PARTY

Trotsky wrote in 1938, 'A revolution is 'made' directly by a minority.'

Who were the Bolsheviks?
The Bolsheviks were founded by Vladimir Lenin and Alexander Bogdanov when the Social Democratic Party *(p.32)* split into two: the Bolsheviks and the Mensheviks. Bolshevik means 'majority' and Menshevik means 'minority'.

When was the Bolshevik party formed?
The Bolsheviks were formed in Brussels, Belgium, in 1903.

How many members did the Bolshevik party have?
At the beginning of 1917, they had just 23,000 members.

What did the Bolshevik party believe in?
The Bolsheviks had 5 main beliefs:
- ☑ In creating a communist society in which all private ownership of property, land and businesses would be abolished to benefit the workers.

- The party should be run by a small dedicated group of revolutionaries who would lead the communist revolution.
- Russia was not ready for a communist revolution according to Marx's theory because it was not yet fully industrialised and the peasants and workers were not ready.
- The Bolsheviks would create a 'Dictatorship of the Proletariat' and rule on the workers' behalf.
- They refused to work with other political parties.

How were the beliefs of the Bolshevik party different to those of the Mensheviks?

There were 3 main differences between the Mensheviks' beliefs and those of the Bolsheviks:

- The Mensheviks were willing to work with other left-wing parties to bring about democracy, but the Bolsheviks were not.
- The Bolsheviks believed in forcing a revolution, whereas the Mensheviks believed in a more democratic approach to gaining power.
- The Mensheviks believed a liberal capitalist society would be a stepping stone to communism, whereas the Bolsheviks believed a small group leading a revolution by force was the way to achieve it.

> **DID YOU KNOW?**
>
> Trotsky was originally a Menshevik for a short time, before crossing over and allying himself with Lenin and the Bolsheviks.

THE MENSHEVIKS

Trotsky said to the Mensheviks in 1917, 'You are pitiful isolated individuals; you are bankrupts; your role is played out. Go where you belong from now on - into the dustbin of history!'

Who were the Mensheviks?

The Mensheviks were founded by Julius Martov when the Social Democratic Party *(p.32)* split into two: the Bolsheviks *(p.32)* and the Mensheviks. Bolshevik means 'majority' and Menshevik means 'minority'.

When were the Mensheviks created?

The Mensheviks were formed in Brussels, Belgium, in 1903.

What were the Mensheviks beliefs?

The Mensheviks had 5 key beliefs:

- In creating a communist society in which all private ownership of property, land and businesses would be abolished to benefit the workers.
- The communist revolution would only happen after Russia industrialised to create a large working class. This would take a long time.
- The party should be be democratic, rather than dominated by a 'revolutionary elite'.
- That the party should work with other political parties to achieve a liberal, capitalist society as the first step towards a communist revolution.
- They gained the support of the working class by promoting policies such as an eight hour working day.

How were the Mensheviks different to the Bolsheviks?

There were 3 main differences between the Mensheviks and the Bolsheviks *(p.32)*:

- They were willing to work with other left-wing parties to bring about democracy whereas the Bolsheviks *(p.32)* were not.
- They believed in a more democratic approach to gaining power whereas the Bolsheviks *(p.32)* believed in forcing a revolution.
- They believed that a liberal capitalist society would be a stepping stone to communism, unlike the Bolsheviks *(p.32)* who believed in a small group leading a revolution by force.

What was the role of the Mensheviks in the 1905 Revolution?

The Mensheviks played 3 main roles in the 1905 Revolution:

- They encouraged workers to set up councils or 'soviets'.
- They were crucial to the set up of the Petrograd Soviet *(p.49)*.
- They played an active role in the state Dumas which were established by Tsar Nicholas II *(p.20)* in response to the 1905 Revolution.

What happened to the Mensheviks?

The Bolsheviks *(p.32)* suppressed the Mensheviks, along with all other political parties, and many Mensheviks went into exile.

DID YOU KNOW?

The Mensheviks became less popular after the October Revolution.

THE OCTOBER MANIFESTO, 1905

The October Manifesto seemed to be a compromise by Tsar Nicholas II, but in reality he remained the autocratic leader.

What was the October Manifesto?

The October Manifesto, or The Manifesto on the Improvement of the State Order, was published by Nicholas II's government and granted certain rights and freedoms to the people of Russia.

When was the October Manifesto published?

The October Manifesto was published on 30th October, 1905 (or 17th October, Old Style).

What was the reason for the October Manifesto?

Tsar Nicholas II *(p.20)* was forced to compromise after the uprisings of 1905. He laid out his reforms in the October Manifesto.

What did the October Manifesto contain?

Nicholas II granted 3 key things in the October Manifesto:

- A parliament, called a Duma *(p.36)*, which would have elected representatives.
- Civil rights for all Russian citizens, including freedom of speech and the right to form political parties and trade unions.
- New laws would be discussed and approved by the Duma *(p.36)*.

What were the results of the October Manifesto?

The publication of the October Manifesto led to 3 key results:

- ☑ An array of political parties were created such as the Octobrists, the Kadets, the Social Democratic Party *(p.32)* and others.
- ☑ Nicholas II passed the Fundamental Laws in April 1906 which established the Duma *(p.36)* and its powers. However, he deliberately limited the powers of the Duma so that it was little more than an advisory body.
- ☑ Many middle class people and liberals were very happy with the reforms the October Manifesto outlined.

> **DID YOU KNOW?**
>
> **By offering certain concessions, Nicholas cleverly divided the discontented groups.**
>
> The liberal middle classes were satisfied with the new power they would receive through the establishment of the state Duma, while peasants were bought off by having their debts eased.

THE FUNDAMENTAL LAWS 1906

The Fundamental Laws sharply curtailed the powers of the new state Duma.

What were the Fundamental Laws?

Tsar Nicholas II *(p.20)* set out his political reforms in the Fundamental Laws.

When were the Fundamental Laws made?

The Fundamental Laws were published in April 1906.

Why did Nicholas II pass the Fundamental Laws?

Tsar Nicholas II *(p.20)* published the Fundamental Laws to reestablish his control over the country after the 1905 Revolution forced him to make compromises in the October Manifesto *(p.34)*.

What did the Fundamental Laws state?

There were 6 key features of the Fundamental Laws:

- ☑ The establishment of the Duma *(p.36)*, which was made up of about 500 delegates, and details of how they would contribute to making laws.
- ☑ The tsar *(p.19)* could close the Duma *(p.36)* at any point.
- ☑ The tsar *(p.19)* could change the electoral system.
- ☑ The Duma's *(p.36)* powers would be limited by the creation of an upper house called the Imperial State Council. The tsar *(p.19)* would select half its members.
- ☑ The tsar *(p.19)* could veto any law the Duma *(p.36)* passed.
- ☑ The tsar *(p.19)* could pass any laws he wanted when the Duma *(p.36)* was not in session.

What was the result of Nicholas II passing the Fundamental Laws?

The result of Nicholas II passing the Fundamental Laws was that the powers of the Duma *(p.36)* were limited and he was back in control.

Get our free app at GCSEHistory.com

THE STATE DUMA

The state Duma was Russia's first elected parliament.

What was the Duma?

To please the liberals, Tsar Nicholas II *(p.20)* allowed a parliament called the Duma to be established. This was his main attempt to restore order following the 1905 Revolution.

When was the Duma created?

The Duma was established by Tsar Nicholas II *(p.20)* in his October Manifesto *(p.34)*, published on 30th October, 1905. After being dismissed for the first time in 1906 it was elected a further three times - twice in 1907 and once in 1912.

What was the Duma's purpose?

The Duma was a parliament which would confirm the laws of the Russian Empire.

What happened to the Duma during the First Word War?

The tsar *(p.19)* took over direct command of the army and dissolved the Duma in 1914. But the war didn't go according to plan and the Duma was recalled a year later. By 1917, it was a main source of opposition to the tsar.

What was Tsar Nicholas II's attitude towards the Duma?

Nicholas II's attitude towards the Duma was mixed:

- ☑ As an autocrat, he disliked the idea of sharing power with the people.
- ☑ He didn't really trust the people to have a say in how the country was run.
- ☑ He saw it as a threat so limited its powers through the Fundamental Laws of 1906.
- ☑ He did, at times, treat it seriously.
- ☑ He saw it primarily as an advisory body, and he made sure that he always had the final say.

DID YOU KNOW?

Men aged over 25 had the right to vote.
Women and people of certain nationalities did not have the right to vote.

FIRST DUMA, 1906

The opening of the first Duma was a historic event.

What was the first Duma?

The first Duma was the very first parliament in the Russian Empire during the reign of Tsar Nicholas II *(p.20)*. It was a historic moment because Russia had never before had an elected parliament.

When did the first Duma exist?

The first Duma existed between 27th April and 8th July, 1906.

What did the first Duma want?

The first Duma wanted 3 key reforms:

- ☑ Land reform, where more land would be taken from the landlords and distributed amongst the people.
- ☑ Political prisoners to be released.
- ☑ The Imperial State Council to be abolished.

Who sat in the first Duma?

The first Duma was made up of 4 main groups:

- ☑ Very few radical left-wing parties because most had boycotted the election.
- ☑ The moderate Constitutional Democrats (Kadets) had the most deputies.
- ☑ The Trudoviks (Labourites) had around 100 deputies.
- ☑ There were a number of smaller parties, including the Octobrists.

What was Nicholas II's reaction to the demands of the first Duma?

Nicholas II was horrified by the demands for reform because he saw them as too radical, so he dissolved the first Duma.

What was the result of Nicholas II dissolving the first Duma?

The liberals were very unhappy when Nicholas II dissolved the first Duma and shut it down. His actions increased their opposition to him.

DID YOU KNOW?

Tsar Nicholas II gave a speech to the delegates of the first Duma in the Winter Palace when it opened.

SECOND DUMA, 1907

The second Duma was just as radical as the short-lived first Duma.

What was the second Duma?

The second Duma was the second parliament while Nicholas II was the tsar *(p.19)* of Russia. It was very short-lived because of its radical demands.

When did the second Duma exist?

The second Duma existed between February and June in 1907.

What did the second Duma want?

The second Duma wanted 2 key reforms:

- ☑ It proposed radical change to the tsarist army.
- ☑ It opposed Stolypin's land reforms.

Who sat in the second Duma?

There were changes to which political parties were present in the second Duma:

- Some Kadets were not allowed to sit in the second Duma because they had criticised the government for closing the first one.
- There were more Octobrists and Social Revolutionaries, and 220 socialists altogether.

What was Nicholas II's reaction to the demands of the second Duma?

Some Kadets were not allowed to sit in the second Duma because they had criticised the government for closing the first one.

What was result of Nicholas II dissolving the second Duma?

The political parties began to realise the Duma *(p.36)* did not have any real power and could not bring about any reform.

> **DID YOU KNOW?**
>
> **The second Duma was closed down because it was seen as too radical.**
>
> As a result, Stolypin changed the rules on who had the right to vote.

THIRD DUMA, 1907 TO 1912

The third Duma was more supportive of the tsar because of changes to the electoral laws.

What was the third Duma?

The third Duma was the third parliament while Nicholas II was the Tsar *(p.19)* of Russia.

When did the third Duma exist?

The third Duma was in session between November 1907 and June 1912.

What laws did the third Duma pass?

The third Duma cooperated with, and supported Nicholas II, far more than the previous two. This meant more laws proposed by Stolypin were passed in the following areas:

- Land reform.
- Social welfare measures.
- Improvements to the military.

Who sat in the third Duma?

The third Duma:

- Was affected by Prime Minister Stolypin's alteration of the electoral system, which gave landowners more voting power so only the richest third of the population could vote.
- Saw more pro-tsar conservative deputies elected, such as the Octobrists, so they and other conservatives had most of the seats.
- Had fewer deputies from non-Russian regions.

What was the response of the political parties to the third Duma?

There were 2 key responses to the changes made to the electoral system and the impact this had on the third Duma:

- ☑ The liberals were very unhappy as they realised Nicholas II and his government would never allow true democracy or give up their autocratic powers.
- ☑ The more radical parties were angered by the changes and more groups began to favour revolution.

> **DID YOU KNOW?**
>
> The third Duma was the only state Duma to last its full five-year term.

FOURTH DUMA, 1912 TO 1917

The Fourth (and final) Duma failed to make Tsar Nicholas bring in political reforms.

What was the fourth Duma?

The fourth Duma was the fourth and final parliament while Nicholas II was the Tsar *(p.19)* of Russia.

When did the fourth Duma exist?

The fourth Duma was in session between November 1912 and February 1917. It was finally closed in October 1917.

Who sat in the fourth Duma?

The fourth Duma was elected using the altered electoral system which gave the richest third of the population more voting power. It was dominated by conservatives, especially the nationalists and right-wing parties.

What did the fourth Duma do?

The fourth Duma faced 3 main problems:

- ☑ It struggled to make much of a difference during the crisis of the First World War.
- ☑ In 1915, a progressive bloc formed, consisting of the centre parties, which tried to make the government and Nicholas II more responsive to the people. It failed.
- ☑ One new member, Alexander Kerensky, would become important after the February 1917 revolution.

When was the fourth Duma shut down?

The fourth Duma opened and closed several times between 1912 and 1917. It was eventually dissolved in February 1917. However, members of the fourth Duma continued to run the country as a part of the Provisional Government *(p.50)* so was finally closed in October 1917.

> **DID YOU KNOW?**
>
> **The state Dumas met in the Tauride Palace in St Petersburg.**
>
> The palace was also used by the Provisional Government and the Petrograd Soviet.

PYOTR (PETER) STOLYPIN

'I must carry through effective measures of reform, and at the same time I must face the revolution, resist it and stop it.' - Pyotr Stolypin, 1906

Who was Pyotr Stolypin?

Pyotr Stolypin was the Prime Minister of Russia, and Minister of Internal Affairs of the Russian Empire from 1906 to his assassination in 1911.

What was Pyotr Stolypin best known for?

Stolypin was known for 6 key actions he took as prime minister:

- His policy of repression after the 1905 Revolution. Stolypin used the police and army to crush the revolutionaries.
- There were thousands of executions by hanging, or 'Stolypin's necktie', between 1906 and 1909.
- In 1906, he reformed farming by introducing a law allowing peasants to leave the commune. It also let them enclose their strips of land into small farms. Stolypin hoped this would help prevent revolution and free up labour for industrialisation.
- He introduced social reform between 1906 and 1912, including doubling spending on health, poor relief and aid for farmers.
- He introduced the Peasant Land Bank in 1906, which gave loans to peasants to buy land.
- In 1907, he changed the system for elections to the Duma *(p.36)* so only the richest third of Russia could vote. He also removed the voting rights of national minorities.

What methods did Pyotr Stolypin use to keep control?

Stolypin was known for using a 'carrot and stick' approach to keep control of Russia. He introduced land and welfare reforms to appease the peasants and workers, but at the same time he violently suppressed all opposition.

How successful were Pyotr Stolypin's policies?

Stolypin was successful in 5 main ways:

- Discontent was reduced. The number of political assassinations decreased from around 1200 to 385 and there were fewer peasant uprisings or strikes.
- Heavy industry increased, with a 50% growth in iron and steel production.
- Private land ownership increased, with peasants leaving the mirs.
- Working conditions in factories improved with the introduction of safety inspectors, and workers benefitted from employee insurance against accidents and sickness.
- His suppression of opposition worked and he was able to crush the 1905 Moscow Uprising.

How did Pyotr Stolypin's policies fail?

Stolypin failed in 5 main ways:

- His policies, in particular land reform, needed more time to work. He was assassinated only 5 years after it was introduced.
- His reforms did not go far enough to improve the living and working conditions of both the peasants and the urban workers.
- Discontent and opposition still existed and there were still strikes and demonstrations.
- His repressive measures created even more resentment.
- Some of his reforms were undermined by Tsar Nicholas II *(p.20)*.

What was Pyotr Stolypin's relationship with Nicholas II?

Stolypin's relationship with Tsar Nicholas II *(p.20)* changed over time:

- Initially, Tsar Nicholas II *(p.20)* had a positive relationship with Stolypin because he successfully suppressed uprisings in Russia.
- Nicholas II did undermine some of Stolypin's reforms on education and improvements in factory conditions.
- There is some evidence that Nicholas II was about to dismiss Stolypin as prime minister just before he was assassinated.

Why was Pyotr Stolypin important?

Pyotr Stolypin was the driving force behind reform after 1905.

How did Pyotr Stolypin die?

Stolypin was assassinated in Kiev on 18th September, 1911.

DID YOU KNOW?

3 facts about Stolypin
- When Tsar Nicholas II offered Stolypin the job of prime minister, he initially said no.
- He was assassinated in Kiev at a celebration marking the emancipation of the serfs.
- Some believe the tsar might have been involved, as the assassin was a police spy and the tsar stopped the investigation into the murder.

LAND REFORM

Land reform was very much needed in Russia.

What were Stolypin's land reforms?

Prime Minister Stolypin introduced a series of land reforms which tried to change the way the peasants farmed.

When did Stolypin's land reforms happen?

Stolypin introduced his agrarian (farming) reforms between 1906 and 1911.

Why were Stolypin's land reforms introduced?

There were 4 main reasons Stolypin brought in land reforms:

- To win the support of the peasants and prevent revolution by reducing support for the left.
- To modernise farming in Russia, which was incredibly backward.
- To encourage peasants to leave their communes and farm independently.
- To increase production and prosperity, which would in turn help to prevent revolution and free up labour for industrialisation. He referred to this policy as a 'wager on the strong'.

What did Stolypin's land reforms change?

There were 3 main changes as a result of the land reforms:

- A Peasants' Land Bank was introduced to replace redemption payments, which were loans from the state. This gave loans to peasants to buy land.

Get our free app at GCSEHistory.com

- ☑ From November 1906, peasants could now leave their communes to farm their own land independently. Communes were peasant communities that owned all the land.
- ☑ There were financial incentives to move to Siberia where there was plenty of land.

What were the results of Stolypin's land reforms?

There were 3 main consequences of the land reforms:

- ☑ By 1917, about 15% of peasants had begun farming independently.
- ☑ About 5 million peasants moved to Siberia between 1900 and 1913. However, about 750,000 came back again.
- ☑ Grain production increased by about 16 tonnes from 1906 to 1913.

What were the problems of Stolypin's land reforms?

There were 3 key issues with the land reforms:

- ☑ Stolypin said it might take 20 years for them to be successful, but he was assassinated after only 5 years.
- ☑ Land reform was not simple. Some peasants may have left the mir (commune) but did not change the way in which they farmed. They still had strips of land scattered across the village and did not use modern methods.
- ☑ By 1917, peasant unrest increased again.

DID YOU KNOW?

Stolypin hoped the land reforms would buy loyalty from the peasants.
He was wrong.

RUSSIFICATION

Russification was brought in as a policy in 1881 after the assassination of Tsar Alexander II.

What was the policy of Russification?

Russification was a policy used by both Nicholas II and the communists to encourage non-Russian minorities to identify as Russian, for example by following the Russian Orthodox religion and speaking the Russian language.

Why did Nicholas II use Russification?

There were 3 main reasons why the policy of Russification was introduced:

- ☑ The different nationalities throughout Russia were difficult to manage.
- ☑ Many did not identify as Russian and their loyalty lay with their local culture and leaders instead of with Moscow.
- ☑ Some nationalities wanted independence, which was a threat.

How did Russia's leaders try to achieve Russification?

There were 10 main methods of Russification:

- ☑ Stolypin ensured that Finland became a full part of the empire in 1906.
- ☑ The Bolsheviks *(p.32)* passed the Decree on Nationalities in 1917.
- ☑ The 1918 constitution formally created the RSFSR which incorporated parts of Central Asia formally into the Empire.
- ☑ The 1924 constitution created the USSR.

Quizzes, amazing exam preparation tools and more at GCSEHistory.com

- The 1936 constitution apparently gave more rights and representation to nationalities, but in reality Stalin had tightened his control.
- The communists allowed nationalities to keep their own governments, but the Sovnarkom *(p.70)* always had the final say in all decisions.
- Children were taught Russian in schools.
- Restricting the practice of minority religions.
- Improving infrastructure so there were better communications between Moscow and the more distant regions of the Empire.
- Repression of uprisings and protests against the regime.

How successful was Russification?

The challenges posed by the different nationalities never went away, but there were 3 key elements of success.

- Nicholas II ensured that different nationalities were represented in the Duma *(p.36)* so that they feel more involved with the political decisions.
- Stalin was able to re-incorporate areas which were lost after the Treaty of Brest-Litovsk *(p.63)*, such as Poland with the Nazi-Soviet Pact.
- The Duma *(p.36)* and constitutions, while they were in reality very limited in the freedoms they granted, placated the nationalities and prevented any mass uprisings.

How did Russification fail?

There were 5 main ways in which the policy of Russification failed:

- Minority protests contributed to the collapse of the Provisional Government *(p.50)*.
- Lenin lost huge areas of the empire with the Treaty of Brest-Litovsk *(p.63)*.
- Many nationalities failed to demonstrate true loyalty to Stalin. For example, Ukrainian peasants were particularly hostile towards collectivisation.
- Many nationalities would continue with their own language and culture in secret despite the restrictions imposed.
- The different nationalities still strived for independence.

DID YOU KNOW?

The assassination of Alexander II was carried out by a group known as 'People's Will'. They wanted to overthrow the autocratic rule of the tsars.

THE LENA GOLDFIELD STRIKE, 1912

The Lena Goldfield strike and massacre had echoes of the 1905 Revolution.

What was the Lena Goldfield Massacre?

The Lena Goldfield Massacre was the killing of goldfield workers who were on strike. The workers were shot by the army. The gold fields were located by the River Lena in Siberia.

When was the Lena Goldfield Massacre?

The Lena Goldfield Massacre happened on 17th April, 1912 (or 4th April, Old Style).

What caused the Lena Goldfield strike?

The goldfield workers went on strike to protest against poor and harsh working conditions.

What did the workers demand during the Lena Goldfield strike?

The workers had 3 main demands:
- ☑ An 8-hour work day.
- ☑ An increase in wages.
- ☑ Better food; they were often given rotten meat.

What was the tsar's response to the Lena Goldfield strike?

The army and police were sent to deal with the strike:
- ☑ The administration refused to agree to the workers' demands.
- ☑ The strike committee and those on strike were arrested.
- ☑ Protestors were shot by the army, with around 270 killed and 250 injured.

What was the people's response to the Lena Goldfield strike?

The massacre sparked more strikes across the Russian Empire, with 700 being held during April 1912. According to Lenin, the Lena massacre 'inflamed the masses with revolutionary fire'.

What was the Duma's response to the Lena Goldfield strike?

The massacre was investigated by the Duma *(p. 36)*. Alexander Kerensky led the investigation and reported on the terrible conditions faced by miners.

Why was the Lena Goldfield strike important?

The Lena Goldfield strike and massacre were important because they showed 2 main things:
- ☑ Working conditions for the working class were still awful.
- ☑ Nicholas II and his government would still use force to crush opposition.

DID YOU KNOW?

The government's reaction to the strike caused horror and outrage across Russia.

It was a clear signal the government had not changed and would continue to use harsh and lethal suppression of all protests.

RUSSIA AND THE FIRST WORLD WAR

Russia mobilised its troops to defend its ally Serbia.

What happened with Russia and the First World War when it joined?

Russia joined with Britain and France in the Triple Entente, against Germany and the Triple Alliance, in the First World War.

When did Russia enter the First World War?

Germany declared war on Russia on 1st August, 1914. Russia ended the war with Germany on 3rd March, 1918.

Why did Russia enter the First World War?

There were 2 key reasons why Russia entered the First World War:

- Austria declared war on Serbia on the 28th July, 1914. Russia mobilised her troops in July to protect Serbia.
- Germany declared war on Russia because Russia refused to stop mobilising her troops.

What was the public response to Russia's entry into the First World War?

There were 3 main initial responses:

- The people of the Russian Empire were very patriotic and supported Nicholas II.
- The Duma *(p.36)* and constitutions, while they were in reality very limited in the freedoms they granted, placated the nationalities and prevented any mass uprisings.
- The tsar *(p.19)* became more popular as the military was initially successful against Germany.

How successful was Russia's military when they entered the First World War?

There were 3 key military defeats:

- Germany defeated Russia at Tannenberg in August 1914.
- Germany defeated Russia at Masurian Lakes in September 1914.
- Russia had done incredibly badly by the end of 1915. The Germans had occupied parts of Russia and 2 million men were dead or injured.

Why did discontent grow when Russia entered the First World War?

There were 3 main reasons for growing discontent connected to the First World War:

- The military defeats and the German occupation.
- The people blamed Nicholas II and his government for the failures and the poor state of the Russian Army which had insufficient supplies.
- The First World War exacerbated the extreme domestic impoverishment.

When did Tsar Nicholas II take command of Russia's army in the First World War?

Tsar Nicholas II *(p.20)* took command of the Russian army and navy in August 1915.

Why did Tsar Nicholas II take command of Russia's war effort during the First World War?

Nicholas II thought it was his duty to take command, especially as the army had suffered several key defeats.

What were the consequences of Tsar Nicholas II taking command of Russia's war effort during the First World War?

The decision of Tsar Nicholas II *(p.20)* to assume command of the Russian Army was widely seen as a mistake for 3 key reasons:

- People now blamed him personally for Russia's military defeats.
- It caused his popularity with the people to decrease.
- He left Tsarina Alexandra *(p.75)* in control as regent and she was extremely unpopular.

DID YOU KNOW?

Tsar Nicholas II and Kaiser Wilhelm II were relatives.
- ✔ They were cousins.
- ✔ They sent each other telegrams in the run up to the First World War breaking out.
- ✔ They were called the 'Willy-Nicky' telegrams.

EFFECTS OF THE FIRST WORLD WAR

The First World War had a devastating impact on Russia.

What were the effects of the First World War on Russia?

Russia suffered massive social, economic and political effects because of the First World War.

What were the economic effects of the First World War on Russia?

The First World War had 5 major economic effects on Russia:

- ✔ The transport system could not cope because it was so archaic. There were few railways or proper roads. The whole system broke down due to the demands of the mobilisation of the army, and transporting weapons, resources and food.
- ✔ The number of men conscripted into the armed forces meant there was a shortage of workers in the factories and on the farms. This led to shortages of goods and food.
- ✔ The national debt increased because the government had to borrow money, and taxes were increased to pay for the war.
- ✔ Russia lost resources when Germany occupied parts of the empire. The impact of this was worsened because Germany also cut off Russia's access to their allies, on whom they relied for imports. These supplies had to come via the port of Vladivostok, which was frozen in winter.
- ✔ The government printed too much paper money, which caused the Russian rouble to fall in value. This led to inflation.

What were the social effects of the First World War on Russia?

There were 4 key social effects of the First World War:

- ✔ Rural areas were stripped of men as they went to fight.
- ✔ There were food shortages because the transport system couldn't cope and food was requisitioned to feed the army.
- ✔ The shortages of goods and food, combined with the government printing more money, led to inflation of 200% by 1916. Working class people struggled as prices rose faster than wages.
- ✔ Unemployment rose in the cities. Demand for goods dropped, and factories could not get the resources they needed due to the collapse of the transport system.

What were the political effects of the First World War on Russia?

There were 5 key political effects of the First World War:

- ✔ There was increased opposition to Nicholas II from the fourth Duma *(p.39)*.
- ✔ Tsarina Alexandra *(p.75)* was made regent when Nicholas II took charge of the army. Her incompetence led to an increase in opposition to the government.

- There was increased criticism of the tsarina because of Rasputin's influence over her and the decisions she made.
- Many historians argue that Nicholas II was greatly weakened by the First World War and that his mistakes, his increased unpopularity and his defeats were the main reasons he fell from power.
- Others argue that Nicholas II would have fallen from power without the First World War, due to the pre-existing social and economic problems, and the political opposition he already faced. The war simply sped things up.

What were the effects of the First World War on the relationship between the tsar and the Duma in Russia?

The First World War ruined the relationship between Tsar Nicholas II *(p.20)* and the fourth Duma *(p.39)* in 4 key ways:

- Nicholas II initially suspended the fourth Duma *(p.39)* against its wishes in August 1914.
- Members criticised Nicholas II's handling of the war and demanded the Duma *(p.36)* had more of a say in how the country and the war was run. Nicholas II refused to make changes.
- In 1915, members of the fourth Duma *(p.39)* created the Progressive Bloc, consisting of the centre parties. It tried to make the government, and Nicholas II, more responsive to the people. It failed.
- The fourth Duma *(p.39)* was very critical of Tsarina Alexandra *(p.75)* and Rasputin.

What were the effects of the First World War on Tsarina Alexandra of Russia?

The First World War changed the position of Tsarina Alexandra *(p.75)* in 4 main ways:

- When Nicholas II took command of the army in August 1915 he made Alexandra his regent. She was now in charge in his absence.
- Alexandra believed in autocracy. She would not work with the fourth Duma *(p.39)* which, as a result, was very critical of her.
- She appointed ministers who were not always competent.
- She became highly criticised by the people because she was German, and because of her decisions as regent and her friendship with Rasputin.

DID YOU KNOW?

Around 15 million men served in the Russian Army during the First World War.

THE FEBRUARY REVOLUTION, 1917

The revolutions of 1917 were triggered by Russia's involvement in the First World War.

What was the February Revolution?

The February Revolution was the first of two revolutions which took place in Russia in 1917. The February Revolution began with strikes and riots over the lack of food.

When was the February Revolution?

The February Revolution is sometimes known as the March Revolution depending on which calendar is used. It took place between 23rd February and 3rd March, 1917, using the old calendar, or between 8th and 16th March, 1917, using the new one.

Where did the February Revolution take place?

The February Revolution of 1917 occurred in Petrograd. Petrograd, located on the Baltic Sea in the north-west of Russia, was called St Petersburg until 1914. It was then renamed, as it was felt the original name was 'too German'. It became Leningrad in 1924, after Lenin's death, and was then renamed St Petersburg once again in 1991.

What caused the February Revolution?

There were several immediate and long-term causes of the February Revolution.

What were the long-term causes of the February Revolution?

There were 4 key long-term causes:

- The discontent caused by the awful living and working conditions of the working class.
- The discontent caused by poverty and the frequent hunger suffered by peasants. There were also continuing issues with land ownership.
- Middle class anger and frustration at not having any real political power.
- The nationalities from the different provinces wanted to be independent from Russian rule.

What were the immediate causes of the February Revolution?

There were 6 key immediate causes of the February Revolution:

- The First World War caused significant disruption to Russia's economy and eroded the support for Nicholas II from the peasants, the working class, the middle class and the upper class.
- Russia was suffering from food and fuel shortages during the winter of 1916-17.
- By January 1917, the morale of the Russian Army was very low with 1.5 million deserting in 1916.
- On 9th February, there were massive strikes in Moscow and Petrograd.
- The strikes increased when, on 19th January, the Petrograd authorities announced bread would be rationed from 1st March.
- There was a huge march in Petrograd on 23rd February, celebrating International Women's Day, which became an anti-government protest against the war and the tsar. *(p. 19)*

What were the key events of the February Revolution?

There were 6 key events during the February Revolution:

- By 25th February, 200,000 people were on strike in Petrograd.
- On 26th February, Nicholas II ordered the fourth Duma *(p.39)* to close down but they refused.
- On 27th February, Nicholas II ordered the army to shoot the protesters. 66,000 soldiers from the Petrograd garrison refused and mutinied, and joined the protesters instead. The Petrograd Soviet *(p.49)*, or workers council, was created.
- On 28th February, the Petrograd Soviet *(p.49)* issued Order Number 1 which stated that the armed forces should only obey the orders of the Soviet. On the same day the sailors in Kronstadt mutinied. At this point, Nicholas II was asked to abdicate.
- On 1st March, the Soviets recognised the authority of the Provisional Government *(p.50)* set up by the fourth Duma *(p.39)* under the leadership of Prince Lvov *(p.79)*.
- Tsar Nicholas II *(p.20)* abdicated on behalf of himself and his son on 2nd March, 1917.

What were the results of the February Revolution?

There were 3 main results of the February Revolution.

- The end of 300 years of Romanov rule and the end of the monarchy.
- This was followed by the end of the empire and the formation of the republic in the spring of 1917.

- The establishment of dual power, or dual authority, between the Russian Provisional Government *(p.50)* and the Petrograd Soviet *(p.49)* of Workers' and Soldiers' Deputies.

Why did the February Revolution succeed?

There were 6 main reasons the February Revolution succeeded:

- The main reason was the army failed to support Tsar Nicholas II *(p.20)* and refused to fire on the protesters. The mutiny meant Nicholas II could no longer rely on the support of the army to prop up his government.
- Aristocrats and key members of his own government lost faith in Nicholas II, withdrew their support, and persuaded Nicholas II to abdicate.
- There was an alternative government to Nicholas II when the fourth Duma *(p.39)* created the Provisional Government *(p.50)*, which was supported by the Petrograd Soviet *(p.49)*.
- Nicholas II was blamed for Russia's failures in the First World War and, as a result, he lost the support of many different social classes including the workers, the middle class and the aristocrats. He was left with little support.
- The shortages caused by the First World War significantly increased the amount of discontent in Russia, so opposition became much more widespread and more dangerous to Nicholas II's position.
- The reputation of the tsar's *(p.19)* government had been fundamentally weakened by the failures in the First World War and the influence Rasputin was reputed to have had over Tsarina Alexandra *(p.75)*.

DID YOU KNOW?

The February Revolution is often described as being 'spontaneous' in the sense that there wasn't just one group who organised it.

THE PETROGRAD SOVIET

A Petrograd Soviet played a very important role in the October Revolution.

What was the Petrograd Soviet?

The Petrograd Soviet was a council of workers' and soldiers' deputies in Russia.

When was the Petrograd Soviet formed?

The Petrograd Soviet was formed on 12th March, 1917.

Who was the founder of the Petrograd Soviet?

The Petrograd Soviet was formed by Leon Trotsky.

Who were the members of the Petrograd Soviet?

The leaders of the Soviet were a mix of radical socialists, Mensheviks and Social Revolutionaries but also a small number of Bolsheviks *(p.32)*. The leadership included Trotsky and Kerensky, who was also a member of the Provisional Government *(p.50)*.

Why was the Petrograd Soviet created?

The Petrograd Soviet was set up because of the massive unrest in Petrograd. Tsar Nicholas II's *(p.20)* government was collapsing and soldiers declared their support for the revolution.

Get our free app at GCSEHistory.com

Why was the Petrograd Soviet important?

The Petrograd Soviet was important for 4 key reasons:

- ✓ It shared power with the Provisional Government *(p.50)*, called the dual authority or dual power, between March 1917 and October 1917.
- ✓ It issued Order Number 1 on 1st March which stated the armed forces should only obey the orders of the Soviet. It should not obey the Provisional Government *(p.50)* if orders from that organisation contradicted or undermined those of the Soviet.
- ✓ It organised the defence of Petrograd during the Kornilov Revolt *(p.54)* in August 1917, using the Red Guard after the Provisional Government *(p.50)* gave them weapons.
- ✓ Trotsky used the Petrograd Soviet to help plan the October Revolution *(p.56)*.

In what ways was the Petrograd Soviet's impact limited?

The Petrograd Soviet's impact was limited in 4 key ways:

- ✓ It was reluctant to take power because there were so many problems in Russia which would be incredibly difficult to solve. They did not want to take responsibility for failing to solve these problems.
- ✓ The Mensheviks in the Petrograd Soviet believed in a socialist revolution but they did not think that Russia was ready for the revolution yet. Therefore, they wanted to fully industrialise first and have a phase where it was controlled by the bourgeoisie or upper class.
- ✓ The Petrograd Soviet was prepared to support the Provisional Government *(p.50)* because it represented the upper class and, by supporting it, the Petrograd Soviet appeared to not prioritise the needs of the workers.
- ✓ It did not want to weaken the Provisional Government *(p.50)* because they feared the tsar *(p.19)* would regain power.

DID YOU KNOW?

The idea of soviets had formed during the 1905 Revolution.

THE PROVISIONAL GOVERNMENT

The Provisional Government lost the support of the people because it made several important mistakes.

What was the Provisional Government?

The Provisional Government was the temporary government set up in Russia after Tsar Nicholas II *(p.20)* abdicated and the tsarist government collapsed.

When was the Provisional Government created?

The Provisional Government was created on 2nd March, 1917.

Who set up the Provisional Government?

The Provisional Government was created by 12 members of the fourth Duma *(p.39)*. The initial leader was Prince Lvov *(p.79)*, a liberal.

Who were the members of the Provisional Government?

The Provisional Government:

- ☑ Consisted of 12 members of the fourth Duma *(p.39)*.
- ☑ Was led by Prince Lvov *(p.79)*, a liberal, from March until July.
- ☑ Was led by Alexander Kerensky, a Socialist Revolutionary, from July until October.
- ☑ The other members were a mixture of Kadets and Octobrists.

What were the weaknesses of the Provisional Government?

The Provisional Government (PG) had 4 key weaknesses:

- ☑ It lacked authority because it shared power with the Petrograd Soviet *(p.49)*.
- ☑ It lacked legitimacy because it didn't represent the people. It was made up of mainly upper class men and was not elected by the population.
- ☑ It lacked power because the Petrograd Soviet's *(p.49)* Order Number One gave the Soviet control of the armed forces.
- ☑ It was not responsible for all areas of government because the Petrograd Soviet *(p.49)* controlled some, such as the transport system and soldiers.

What were the key actions of the Provisional Government?

The Provisional Government took 3 key actions:

- ☑ On 3rd March 1917, it published its eight principles of government including complete political and religious amnesty which allowed political prisoners to be released from prison, freedom of speech, and the setting up of a Constituent Assembly *(p.62)*.
- ☑ It published a set of decrees including an eight hour working day, minimum wage, the abolition of the death sentence and the confiscation of all Crown lands.
- ☑ It launched the June Offensive *(p.52)* which was unsuccessful and led to the loss of 400,000 men and mutinies. Kerensky, the Minister of War, was blamed and it led to more social unrest.

What mistakes did the Provisional Government make?

The Provisional Government made 5 key mistakes:

- ☑ It continued the war with Germany. It had little choice as the Allies threatened to cut off financial aid if Russia pulled out of the war.
- ☑ It did not successfully deal with the issue of shortages of food and goods. Its economic measures, such as an increase in income tax, were just ignored.
- ☑ It did not address the needs of the peasants. They wanted more land from the landlords but the Provisional Government did nothing because, in reality, it had little control over most of Russia and it would cost too much money.
- ☑ The Provisional Government introduced decrees which increased people's rights, including the ability to criticise its actions.
- ☑ It did not arrange elections, which made it seem the Provisional Government wanted to keep its power.

What are historians' opinions on the effectiveness of the Provisional Government rule Russia in 1917?

Historians debate how effectively the Provisional Government ruled Russia during its brief time in power.

How was the Provisional Government effective?

There were 4 main ways that the Provisional Government ruled Russia effectively:

- ☑ It appealed to the people through its liberal approach. Its key principles included freedom of speech, the release of political prisoners and the abolition of the death sentence.
- ☑ It passed decrees to improve working conditions including a minimum wage and an eight hour working day.
- ☑ It always intended to set up a Constituent Assembly *(p.62)* which would provide democratic elections.
- ☑ They effectively dealt with the riots and uprisings during the July Days and the Kornilov revolt *(p.54)*.

How was the Provisional Government ineffective?

There were 9 main ways the Provisional Government was ineffective in ruling Russia:

- ☑ It never really achieved full authority over the country because it had to share power with the Petrograd Soviet *(p.49)*.
- ☑ The Petrograd Soviet *(p.49)* had control of the army due to Order Number One.
- ☑ It was unelected and didn't really represent the people as it was mainly made up of aristocrats.
- ☑ It was responsible for the disastrous June Offensive *(p.52)* where 400,000 men were lost.
- ☑ It failed to deal with the problems of hunger and had to bring in food rationing.
- ☑ It was reliant on the Petrograd Soviet *(p.49)* and the Bolsheviks *(p.32)* to put down the Kornilov revolt *(p.54)*.
- ☑ It failed to deal with land distribution which was the main grievance for the Russian peasants.
- ☑ It failed to pull Russia out of the war, which meant it failed to solve many of the problems which caused the downfall of the tsar *(p.19)* in the first place.
- ☑ The increase in support for the Bolsheviks *(p.32)* demonstrates how unpopular the Provisional Government became. Their famous slogan, "Peace, Land, Bread", represented the key areas where the Provisional Government failed to deliver.

DID YOU KNOW?

The Provisional Government was only intended to be in power until elections could be organised for a more permanent, democratic solution.

THE JUNE OFFENSIVE, 1917

The June Offensive was the Provisional Government's major push to win the First World War. It failed.

What was the June Offensive?

The June Offensive was a Russian attack to push back the Austro-Hungarians and Germans to win the war. It was a disaster. It is also known as the July Offensive depending on which calendar you are using.

When did the June Offensive take place?

The June Offensive began on 18th June, 1917 and had collapsed by 5th July, 1917 by the old calendar. By the new calendar it began on 1st July, 1917.

Why did the June Offensive occur?

The June Offensive was launched as an attempt by Russia to achieve a crushing military victory and end the war.

Who organised the June Offensive?

As the Minister for War, it was Alexander Kerensky who organised the June Offensive.

What were the results of the June Offensive?

There were 3 key results of the June Offensive:

- ☑ Huge losses of 400,000 men. It also led to mutinies and chaos.
- ☑ Both the Provisional Government *(p.50)* and Kerensky, as the minister of war, were blamed for the failures in the war. This led to resignations, especially from the Kadets.

- ☑ The July Days were a period of social, economic and political upheaval in Russia while the Provisional Government *(p.50)* was in charge.

> **DID YOU KNOW?**
>
> The June Offensive is also known as the Kerensky Offensive, after its leader Alexander Kerensky.

THE JULY DAYS, 1917

The Provisional Government managed to survive the July Days and restore its reputation but it was only a temporary reprieve.

What were the July Days in Russia?
The July Days were a period of social, economic and political upheaval in Russia while the Provisional Government *(p.50)* was in power.

When were the July Days in Russia?
The July Days happened between 3rd and 7th July, 1917.

Why did the July Days happen in Russia?
There were 3 key reasons for the July Days uprising:
- ☑ Bread rationing was brought in by the Provisional Government *(p.50)* due to shortages in March 1917. By July these food shortages had worsened.
- ☑ The June Offensive *(p.52)* had totally failed and people were war weary.
- ☑ The Bolsheviks *(p.32)*, under Lenin, had very successful anti-Provisional Government *(p.50)* propaganda.

What happened during the July Days in Russia?
There were 6 key events during the July Days uprising:
- ☑ Workers, soldiers and Kronstadt sailors protested in Petrograd.
- ☑ The Bolshevik *(p.32)* Party organised riots. The crowds used the Bolshevik slogans of 'Peace, Bread and Land', and 'All Power to the Soviets'.
- ☑ The Petrograd Soviet *(p.49)* rejected a demand for them to take control.
- ☑ The Provisional Government *(p.50)*, with the help of loyal troops, cleared the streets and regained control.
- ☑ Bolshevik *(p.32)* leaders, including Trotsky, were rounded up and 800 members were arrested and imprisoned.
- ☑ Lenin fled to Finland and the reputation of the Bolsheviks *(p.32)* was in tatters.

Who was involved with the July Days In Russia?
The protests during the July Days involved the following groups: revolutionaries, sailors, soldiers, Bolsheviks *(p.32)* and workers.

What were the results of the July Days in Russia?
There were 3 key results of the July Days:
- ☑ The Provisional Government's *(p.50)* reputation was restored.

Get our free app at GCSEHistory.com

- ☑ The opponents of the Provisional Government *(p.50)* were imprisoned or had fled abroad, e.g. Lenin.
- ☑ Kerensky became the leader of the Provisional Government *(p.50)* and worked with the Kadets and Socialists.

> **DID YOU KNOW?**
>
> **Alexander Kerensky became the leader of the Provisional Government after the July Days crsis.**
>
> He was both a member of the Provisional Government and the Petrograd Soviet.

THE KORNILOV REVOLT, 1917

General Kornilov was appointed to restore discipline in the army, yet led a revolt by the army.

What was the Kornilov Revolt?

The Kornilov Revolt, or the Kornilov Coup, was an unsuccessful coup by part of the army against the Russian Provisional Government *(p.50)* and the Petrograd Soviet *(p.49)*.

Who was the leader of the Kornilov Revolt?

General Lavr Kornilov was Commander-in-Chief of the Russian Army from July to September 1917. He was the leader of the Kornilov Revolt.

When was the Kornilov Revolt?

It happened from 27th to 30th August, 1917, using the old calendar. (In the new calendar, 10th to 13th September, 1917).

Why did the Kornilov Revolt happen?

There are 2 main reasons why the Kornilov Revolt occurred:

- ☑ Prime Minister Kerensky aimed to improve army discipline so that Russia could win the First World War. He appointed General Kornilov as the commander-in-chief of the army to bring about this change.
- ☑ General Kornilov wanted Kerensky to declare martial law and close down the soviets. Kerensky refused and sacked Kornilov who reacted by sending troops to Petrograd.

What happened during the Kornilov Revolt?

There were 4 key events during the Kornilov Revolt:

- ☑ On 24th August, General Kornilov ordered troops to Petrograd to close down the Petrograd Soviet *(p.49)*.
- ☑ Kerensky called on the Petrograd Soviet *(p.49)* to defend the city and allowed them to arm the Red Guard and in return he freed the Bolshevik *(p.32)* prisoners arrested in the July Days uprising.
- ☑ General Kornilov's route into the city was blocked by railway workers.
- ☑ The Bolsheviks *(p.32)* stopped General Kornilov and he was arrested on 1st September, 1917.

What were the results of the Kornilov Revolt?

The Kornilov Revolt affected the government and had 5 other important consequences:

- ☑ It weakened the position of the Provisional Government *(p.50)*. They lost support from the right-wing because they had given weapons to the Bolsheviks *(p.32)*. They lost support from the left-wing because Kerensky had tried to compromise with Kornilov at first.

- ✓ The Bolsheviks *(p.32)* had more support because they had defended Petrograd from General Kornilov and now they had weapons.
- ✓ Membership of the Bolshevik *(p.32)* Party increased by about 100,000 by October.
- ✓ Because their position was strengthened, the Bolsheviks *(p.32)* were able to gain control of the Petrograd Soviet *(p.49)* by September 1917.
- ✓ Morale and discipline in the army decreased even more.

> **DID YOU KNOW?**
>
> **General Kornilov was captured by Austrians during the First World War.**
> However, he managed to escape and returned to Russia.

GROWTH IN SUPPORT FOR BOLSHEVIK PARTY

The key Bolshevik slogan was 'Peace, Land, Bread.'

What was the Bolshevik growth in support?

There was a growth in support for the Bolshevik *(p.32)* Party between February and October 1917, during the period when the Provisional Government *(p.50)* was in charge of Russia.

When was the growth in support for the Bolsheviks?

The growth in support for the Bolsheviks *(p.32)* was between February and October 1917. In particular, there was a spurt in their growth during the summer after the Kornilov Revolt *(p.54)*.

Who supported the Bolshevik Party that led to a growth in its support?

Many soldiers, sailors and workers supported the Bolshevik *(p.32)* Party.

Why did the Bolsheviks see a growth in support?

There were 6 key reasons why support for the Bolsheviks *(p.32)* grew:

- ✓ Lenin's influence was considerable. His personality and determination encouraged other Bolsheviks *(p.32)* to follow his lead.
- ✓ Lenin's 'April Theses' promised key things to key groups. 'Peace, Land and Bread' appealed to soldiers, peasants and workers.
- ✓ People's desperation to end the First World War was a key factor in the growth of Bolshevik support.
- ✓ Bolshevik *(p.32)* newspapers spread their propaganda messages.
- ✓ The Provisional Government *(p.50)* became more unpopular after the Kornilov Revolt *(p.54)* whereas the Bolsheviks *(p.32)* became more popular as they were seen as the defenders of Petrograd.
- ✓ The Bolsheviks *(p.32)* were able to build the Red Guards, a private Bolshevik army, led by Leon Trotsky and arm them with the weapons given to them during the Kornilov Revolt *(p.54)*.

> **DID YOU KNOW?**
>
> Lenin returned to Russia in April 1917 with the help of the Germans.

THE OCTOBER REVOLUTION, 1917

The October Revolution was a revolution led by a small, dedicated group of revolutionaries.

What was the October Revolution?

The October Revolution is sometimes called the November Revolution due to Russia using a different calendar. It was the Bolshevik-led *(p.32)* revolution to remove the Provisional Government *(p.50)* from power.

When was the October Revolution?

The October Revolution occurred on 25th and 26th October, 1917, according to the old calendar. The dates are 7th and 8th November, 1917, under the new calendar.

Who led the October Revolution?

The October Revolution was organised by the Bolsheviks *(p.32)*, led by Lenin. Leon Trotsky played a major role in organising the revolution.

Why did the October Revolution happen?

There were 5 key reasons why the October Revolution occurred:

- There was a shift in power and popularity from the Provisional Government *(p.50)* to the Petrograd Soviet *(p.49)* after the Kornilov Revolt *(p.54)*.
- On 10th October, Lenin returned to Russia and was able to persuade leading Bolsheviks *(p.32)* that the party should plan for an armed uprising against the Provisional Government *(p.50)*.
- On 16th October, Trotsky, as the leader of the Petrograd Soviet *(p.49)*, created the Military Revolutionary Committee. This gained the support of the Peter and Paul Fortress, so the Bolsheviks *(p.32)* had the support of the military.
- On 24th October, the leader of the Provisional Government *(p.50)*, Kerensky, attempted to limit the power of the Bolsheviks *(p.32)* by ordering their arrest and stopping their newspapers. Trotsky used the Military Revolutionary Committee to take over key bridges and the telephone exchange.
- Lenin needed to act before the elections to the Constituent Assembly *(p.62)* which were scheduled for November 1917.

What happened during the October Revolution?

There were 3 key events during the actual takeover:

- Early in the morning of 24th-25th October, the Red Guards took control of banks, government buildings and the railway stations.
- In the evening of 25th October, the Red Guards entered the Winter Palace *(p.57)* and arrested the members of the Provisional Government *(p.50)* that were present.
- On 26th October, Lenin announced a new communist government called the Council of the People's Commissars.

Why were the Bolsheviks successful during the October Revolution?

There were 5 key reasons why the Bolsheviks *(p.32)* were successful during the October Revolution:

- Trotsky played a key role in the success of the October Revolution. He cleverly used his position as the elected leader of the Petrograd Soviet *(p.49)*, created the Military Revolutionary Committee, and helped increase support for the Bolsheviks *(p.32)*.
- The Provisional Government *(p.50)* was weak because it had lost support from all parts of society. The armed forces were crumbling because of the First World War. The peasants felt neglected as their issues had not been addressed.
- Lenin's 'April Theses' appealed to the people, was clear to understand and helped to persuade other leading Bolsheviks *(p.32)* not to support the Provisional Government *(p.50)*. His planning of the uprising was successful.
- They were funded by Germany which helped pay for their propaganda. The Germans hoped that the revolution would be successful so that Russia would pull out of the First World War.

☑ The Bolsheviks *(p.32)* had the support of the major industrial cities.

> **DID YOU KNOW?**
>
> In 1917, Lenin claimed 'It is much easier to shout, abuse and howl than to attempt to relate, to explain.'

STORMING THE WINTER PALACE, OCTOBER 1917
The Winter Palace was used by the Provisional Government.

What was the Storming of the Winter Palace?
Members of the Red Guard and Kronstadt sailors stormed the Winter Palace. The tsars had ruled from there for centuries, and the Provisional Government *(p.50)* also ruled from the palace.

When was the Winter Palace stormed?
It took place on 25th-26th October, 1917, using the old calendar, or on 8th-9th November, 1917, using the new one.

What did the ship Aurora do to the Winter Palace?
Aurora, a cruiser harboured nearby, fired blank shots to signal the start of the attack.

What was the aftermath of the Storming of the Winter Palace?
Some members of the Provisional Government *(p.50)* were arrested when the palace was stormed, although Alexander Kerensky escaped and fled. The Bolsheviks *(p.32)* claimed they were now in power.

> **DID YOU KNOW?**
>
> **There was no resistance to the Bolsheviks when they stormed the Winter Palace.**
>
> More people were injured in a 1920 reenactment of the storming of the Winter Palace than in the real event.

BOLSHEVIK CONSOLIDATION OF POWER
Bolsheviks had very little control over most of Russia after the October Revolution 1917. They had to expand that control to all parts of the country.

What was the Bolshevik consolidation of power?
The Bolshevik consolidation of power was a period of time in which the Bolsheviks *(p.32)* increased their control from just Moscow and Petrograd to most of Russia.

When did the Bolshevik consolidation of power happen?

The Bolshevik consolidation of power was between 1917 and 1921.

How did the Bolsheviks consolidate their growth in power?

There were 6 main actions that the Bolsheviks *(p.32)* took to consolidate their power:

- They issued several decrees between October and December 1917, including the Decree On Peace, the Decree on Land, the Decree on Nationalities and the Decree on Workers' Rights.
- The Bolsheviks *(p.32)* shut down the Constituent Assembly *(p.62)* in January 1918.
- In March 1918, they signed the Treaty of Brest-Litovsk *(p.63)* which ended the war with Germany.
- They fought and won the civil war against the Whites and the Greens between 1918 and 1921.
- They began the Red Terror *(p.67)* by rounding up and executing thousands of their opponents.
- They brought in censorship and by 1921 had closed down all other political parties.

How did the Decree on Land help with the consolidation of the Bolsheviks' power?

The Bolsheviks *(p.32)* issued the Decree on Land in October 1917, which abolished private ownership, including land owned by the tsar *(p.19)*, the Church and private landowners. It was given to the peasants in the hope they would support the Bolsheviks.

How did the Decree on Peace help with the consolidation of Bolshevik power?

The Decree on Peace of October 1917, called for peace to be negotiated between all countries at war. Pulling Russia out of the war would mean the Bolsheviks *(p.32)* could concentrate on establishing a government and consolidating their power.

How did the Decrees on Workers' Rights help with the consolidation of Bolshevik power?

The Decrees on Workers' Rights, issued in November 1917, focused on improvements to working conditions such as pay and unemployment benefits, and put the factories under the control of the workers in the hope the workers would support them.

How did the Decree on Nationalities help with the consolidation of the Bolsheviks' growth in power?

The Decree on Nationalities issued in October 1917, stated that the different nationalities could govern themselves. This was issued in the hope that they would not use the collapse of the tsarist government to gain their independence.

How did closing the Constituent Assembly help with the consolidation of Bolshevik power?

By closing down the Constituent Assembly *(p.62)* on 6th January, 1918, Lenin prevented it being a source of opposition to the Bolsheviks *(p.32)*. He was able to ban all political parties.

DID YOU KNOW?

When the Bolsheviks took power, they made propaganda posters which mocked Tsar Nicholas II for his command of the Russian Army.

DECREE ON LAND, 1917

The Land Decree was passed to win the support of the peasants.

What was the Decree on Land?

The Decree on Land nationalised all land and was issued by the Bolsheviks *(p.32)*. In other words, land was taken away from private landowners, the tsar *(p.19)*, and the Russian Orthodox Church and given to the peasants. No one was allowed to own land.

When was the Decree on Land passed?

The Decree on Land was passed in October 1917.

Who passed the Decree on Land?

The Bolsheviks *(p.32)* passed the Decree on Land.

Why was the Decree on Land issued?

The Decree on Land was passed because Lenin and the Bolsheviks *(p.32)* hoped that winning the support of the peasants would ensure a supply of food for the workers in the cities and towns.

What was the impact of the Decree on Land?

There were two main effects of the Decree on Land:

- In reality, the peasants had already been seizing land so the Decree on Land just legalised their actions.
- The land went to those who were farming it, so some of the poorer peasants, who hadn't farmed any land, were disadvantaged by the reforms.

DID YOU KNOW?

Peasants had already taken the land off the landowners before the Land Decree was announced.

DECREE ON PEACE, 1917

The Peace Decree would pull Russia out of the First World War.

What was the Decree on Peace?

The Decree on Peace demanded immediate peace negotiations between all countries fighting in the First World War. It stated that Russia wanted an immediate ceasefire and to start peace talks with Germany.

When was the Decree on Peace passed?

The Decree on Peace was passed in October 1917.

Who passed the Decree on Peace?

The Bolsheviks *(p.32)* passed the Decree on Peace.

Why was the Decree on Peace issued?

There were 2 main reasons why the Decree on Peace was passed:

- ✔ Lenin hoped communist revolutions would occur across Europe. Therefore, Germany would either be willing to negotiate a fair peace in which Russia would not lose any land nor have to pay reparations, or collapse and the negotiations would be abandoned.
- ✔ Lenin needed to pull out of the First World War so the Bolsheviks *(p.32)* could concentrate on gaining control of Russia.

What was the impact of the Decree on Peace?

There were 3 main effects of the Decree on Peace:

- ✔ The Decree on Peace led to the Bolsheviks *(p.32)* negotiating the Treaty of Brest-Litovsk *(p.63)* with Germany, which was signed on 3rd March, 1918.
- ✔ The Treaty involved making huge concessions to the Germans, giving them large areas of land and promising to pay them reparations.
- ✔ The Treaty was so hated it became one of the causes of the Russian Civil War *(p.65)*.

DID YOU KNOW?

Germany had secretly funded Lenin's return to Russia in the hope that there would be a revolution in Russia and the country would withdraw from the First World War.

DECREE ON WORKERS' RIGHTS, 1917

The Workers' Decrees were passed to win the support of the workers.

What were the Decrees on Workers' Rights?

The Decrees on Workers' Rights attempted to improve working conditions for industrial workers and give them control over the means of production instead of the business owners.

When were the Decrees on Workers' Rights passed?

The Decrees on Workers' Rights were passed in November 1917.

Who passed the Decrees on Workers' Rights?

The Bolsheviks *(p.32)* passed the Decrees on Workers' Rights.

Why were the Decrees on Workers' Rights issued?

The Bolsheviks *(p.32)* passed the Decrees on Workers' Rights to improve working conditions of the workers so they would win their support.

What did the Decrees on Workers' Rights state?

The Decrees on Workers' Rights contained 3 key decrees:

- ✔ In November 1917, the Decree on Work stated there would be an eight-hour day and a maximum 48-hour week.
- ✔ The Decree on Unemployment introduced insurance for all workers against illness, unemployment or injury.

- ☑ The Decree on Workers' Control was issued in December 1917, and handed over the running of all factories to the workers.

What were the positive impacts of the Decrees on Workers' Rights?
The positive impact of the decrees was that they gave the workers many rights they previously did not have.

What were the negative impacts of the Decrees on Workers' Rights?
There were 3 main problems with the Decrees on Workers' Rights because there was little money to support them:
- ☑ Workers gave themselves massive pay rises.
- ☑ Workers sacked or, in some cases, even killed managers.
- ☑ Production levels fell.

> **DID YOU KNOW?**
> The decree stated 'All the laws restricting the work of factory, shop and other committees, or Soviets of workers and employees are hereby annulled.'

DECREE ON NATIONALITIES, 1917
The Nationalities Decree was passed to win support of the different nationalities that made up the Russian Empire.

What was the Decree on Nationalities?
The Decree on Nationalities was a decree which promised the different nationalities within the Russian Empire that they had the right to a government of their own choice. In other words, the Bolsheviks (p.32) would not try to rule them.

When was the Decree on Nationalities passed?
The Decree on Nationalities was passed in October 1917.

Who passed the Decree on Nationalities?
The Decree on Nationalities was issued by the Bolsheviks (p.32).

Why was the Decree on Nationalities issued?
The Decree on Nationalities was issued for two key reasons:
- ☑ To try to win support for the Bolshevik (p.32) revolution from the different ethnic minorities in the Russian Empire.
- ☑ It was hoped the decree would mean the different nationalities would not break away from Russian control.

> **DID YOU KNOW?**
> **After the October Revolution, many regions in Russia declared independence.**
> - ✓ The Ukraine declared its independence in November 1917.
> - ✓ Finland declared its independence on 6th December 1917.

Get our free app at GCSEHistory.com

DECLARATION OF THE RIGHTS OF THE PEOPLES OF RUSSIA, 1917

The Declaration set out the rights of the people. The Bolsheviks did not uphold any of them.

What was the Declaration of the Rights of the Peoples of Russia?

The Declaration of the Rights of the Peoples of Russia promised equality and self-determination for national minorities in an attempt to bond the various regions to the Soviet Union.

When was the Declaration of the Rights of the People signed in Russia?

The Declaration of the Rights of the Peoples of Russia was signed on 15th November, 1917.

Who signed the Declaration of the Rights of the People signed in Russia?

The Declaration of the Rights of the Peoples of Russia was signed by Lenin and Stalin.

Was the Declaration of the Rights of the People in Russia ever respected?

The Soviet Union did not uphold human rights because it was a one-party dictatorship of the Communist Party. All freedoms granted were in name only - the communist government would always have the final say and there was no democratic representation.

DID YOU KNOW?

Estimates on the number of deaths under the communist regime vary.

Some historians claim up to 20 million Soviet citizens were killed by the actions of the Soviet Union.

THE CONSTITUENT ASSEMBLY, 1918

The Constituent Assembly was to be tasked with deciding the new constitution and system of government for Russia. It was shut down on its second day.

What was the Constituent Assembly?

The Constituent Assembly was an elected body organised by the Provisional Government *(p.50)* for the purpose of establishing a new government after the collapse of the tsarist government. It would write a new constitution outlining how Russia would be governed.

When was the Constituent Assembly open?

The Constituent Assembly opened on 5th January and was closed down on 6th January, 1918.

Who closed down the Constituent Assembly?

Lenin closed the Constituent Assembly with the Red Guard. It was done at gunpoint.

Why was the Constituent Assembly closed down?

The Constituent Assembly was closed for 2 main reasons:

- ✅ The results for the Constituent Assembly were not in the Bolsheviks *(p.32)*' favour as the Socialist Revolutionaries gained 57%-58% of the vote. This meant it was not under the control of the Bolsheviks.
- ✅ The Constituent Assembly rejected a proposal from the Sovnarkom *(p.70)* which included all their decrees on land, peace and workers' rights, and a statement which gave all power to the Soviets.

What were the election results for the Constituent Assembly?

The results for the Constituent Assembly are disputed because the elections were interrupted and not all votes were returned. Socialist Revolutionaries won 57-58% of the vote, the Bolsheviks *(p.32)* won 25%, the Kadets won 5% and the Mensheviks won 3%.

> **DID YOU KNOW?**
> Lenin closed down the Constituent Assembly at gunpoint, claiming it was elected on an electoral register that did not fully represent the people.

THE TREATY OF BREST-LITOVSK, MARCH 1918

Lenin described the Treaty of Brest-Litovsk as, 'that abyss of defeat, dismemberment, enslavement and humiliation.'

What was the Brest-Litovsk Peace Treaty?

The Treaty of Brest-Litovsk ended Russia's role in the First World War. The treaty was signed at German-controlled Brest-Litovsk after two months of negotiations.

When was the Brest-Litovsk treaty signed?

The Treaty of Brest-Litovsk was signed on 3rd March, 1918.

Who signed the Brest-Litovsk Treaty?

The treaty was between the new Bolshevik *(p.32)* government of Russia and the Central Powers - the German Empire, Austria-Hungary, Bulgaria and the Ottoman Empire.

Where was the Brest-Litovsk Treaty signed?

The Treaty of Brest-Litovsk was signed at the German Army's headquarters in Brest-Litovsk, which at that time was part of Poland. It is in modern Belarus.

Why did the Bolsheviks agree to sign the Brest-Litovsk Treaty?

There were 6 main reasons why the Bolsheviks *(p.32)* agreed to sign the treaty:

- ✅ They had staked everything, and won all their support, on the promise of immediate withdrawal from the war.
- ✅ The Bolsheviks *(p.32)* agreed to sign because they needed a swift end to war; Russia was not able to defeat Germany.
- ✅ If Russia lost the war, it would mean the end of the Bolshevik *(p.32)* revolution.
- ✅ They believed Germany and the rest of Europe would also have communist revolutions, which would result in the treaty being overturned.
- ✅ Their priority was dealing with opposition to the Bolshevik *(p.32)* revolution inside Russia, and they feared a civil war would begin.
- ✅ They could not afford to fight Germany and a civil war at the same time.

Get our free app at GCSEHistory.com

What was the outcome of the Brest-Litovsk Treaty?

There were 3 main terms of the treaty.

- Russia lost Finland, Estonia, Latvia, Lithuania, Ukraine, Georgia, and parts of Poland from its empire - this was more than a quarter of its farmland and railroads.
- It lost 26% of its population, or 62 million people.
- Germany imposed reparations, or compensation, of 300 million roubles.

What was the impact of the Treaty of Brest-Litovsk on Russia and the Bolshevik Party?

There were 4 main effects of the Treaty of Brest-Litovsk on Russia and the Bolshevik *(p.32)* Party:

- It was considered a humiliation so people were furious with the Bolshevik *(p.32)* Party for signing it.
- The land that Russia lost to Germany was some of the best farmland it had, so food shortages worsened.
- This led to mass migration of people from the towns and cities to the countryside in the search for food.
- Many right-wing people and tsarists were so horrified by the treaty that they were even more determined to oppose the Bolsheviks *(p.32)*. This led to the civil war.

DID YOU KNOW?

The Russia delegates were told to drag out the peace negotiations.

Lenin was hoping that communist revolution would spread across Europe leading to the end of the First World War. He instructed the Russian delegates to make the peace negotiations with the Germans last longer. It wasn't until the Germans restarted the fighting on the Eastern Front, that the Russians signed the Treaty.

THE COMMUNIST PARTY, 1918

The Bolsheviks changed their name to the Communist Party.

What was the Communist Party?

Soon after seizing power in Petrograd in November 1917, the Bolsheviks *(p.32)* began to refer to themselves as communists.

When did the Bolsheviks became the Communist Party?

The Russian Communist Party was named in March 1918.

What did the Communist Party believe in?

The Communist Party held 3 main beliefs:

- The theory of communism of Karl Marx.
- This theory stated that there would be a revolution in which the workers would rise up and abolish the private ownership of land, property and business.
- Power would be in the hands of the workers and would be run for the benefit of the workers.

> **DID YOU KNOW?**
>
> The Communist Party of the Soviet Union was in power until 1991.

THE CIVIL WAR, 1918-1921

The Bolsheviks winning the Russian Civil War centralised their control of the country and their own party.

What was the Russian Civil War?

A civil war was triggered by opposition to the Bolsheviks *(p.32)* from various groups, including monarchists who wanted the tsar *(p.19)* back in power, anti-communists, groups angered by Brest-Litovsk and different nationalities who wanted their independence.

When was the Russian Civil War?

The Russian Civil War took place from 1918 to 1921.

Who fought in the Russian Civil War?

The Russian Civil War was fought between communist (Red) and anti-communist (White) forces. In addition, a number of countries, including Britain and the USA, sent troops to support the Whites. The Reds won.

What were the different armies involved in the Russian Civil War?

There were 3 main groups involved:

- The Red Army, who were the Bolsheviks *(p.32)* or communists.
- The White Army, made up of nationalists and monarchists.
- The Green Army was formed by the peasants.

What were the causes of the Russian Civil War?

There were 5 key reasons why the Russian Civil War happened:

- The Russian Empire had collapsed because many nationalities wanted independence and the Bolshevik *(p.32)* Decree on Nationalities allowed this. People who were pro-Empire wanted to re-conquer these areas.
- Political opposition had grown towards the Bolsheviks *(p.32)* from the Social Revolutionaries, the Mensheviks, the Constituent Assembly *(p.62)*, and the anti-Bolshevik alliance to form the Whites. People objected to the fact the Bolsheviks had seized power undemocratically.
- The Allies were opposed to the Bolsheviks *(p.32)* pulling out of the First World War and the signing of the Treaty of Brest-Litovsk *(p.63)*. They hoped that by supporting the Whites, the Bolsheviks would be defeated and Russia would re-enter the war.
- Law and order had broken down.
- Food requisitioning by the Bolsheviks *(p.32)* angered the peasants and so they formed the Green Army to defend their homes.

What were the consequences of the Russian Civil War on international relations?

The Russian Civil War had 3 main consequences for international relations:

- ✓ It increased the Soviet Union's suspicion that the capitalist West would always seek to overthrow communism.
- ✓ In order to protect the USSR from future foreign interference, Lenin, the leader of the USSR, pursued a policy of worldwide communist revolution.
- ✓ This in turn caused a 'Red Scare' in 1920s America as many feared the worldwide spread of communism.

Who fought against the Bolsheviks in the Russian Civil War?

There were 3 main groups that opposed the Bolsheviks *(p.32)*:

- ✓ The Whites consisted of lots of different groups such as Socialist Revolutionaries, tsarists/monarchists, Liberals, ultra-conservatives, and army officers against the Treaty of Brest-Litovsk *(p.63)*.
- ✓ The Greens consisted of peasants and deserters from other armies.
- ✓ Foreign countries also intervened in the civil war against the Bolsheviks *(p.32)*. Britain, Japan and USA all interfered.

What were the key events of the Russian Civil war?

There were 9 key events during the Russian Civil War:

- ✓ Trotsky became the Commissar for War for the Bolsheviks *(p.32)* and took charge of the Red Army on 13th March, 1918.
- ✓ In May 1918, the Czech Legion rebelled against the Red Army. They were leaving Russia when Trotsky demanded their weapons. They responded by allying with the Socialist Revolutionaries and taking over parts of the Trans-Siberian Railway.
- ✓ On 17th July, 1918, Tsar Nicholas II *(p.20)* and his family were executed in Yekaterinburg to prevent the Whites and the Czech Legion from rescuing them and using them as a rallying point in the Civil War.
- ✓ In August 1918, Trotsky increased the harsh discipline in the Red Army so that one in every ten soldiers was shot if he retreated.
- ✓ The Bolsheviks *(p.32)* suffered a major set-back during the Eastern Front Offensive led by one of the White's leaders, Admiral Kolchak. He attacked in June 1918. However, the Red Army managed to force the Whites to retreat by June 1919.
- ✓ By October 1919, the Red Army had managed to stop General Yudenich's advance on Petrograd and General Denikin's advance on Moscow.
- ✓ Between April and October 1920, the Bolsheviks *(p.32)* were also at war with Poland until they signed the Treaty of Riga in October.
- ✓ The Whites were finally defeated at the Battle of Perekop between 7th and 15th November, 1920.
- ✓ In 1921, the Green Army, led by General Makhno, was finally defeated in the Ukraine and by General Antonov in Tambov where about 50,000 peasants had led an uprising against the Bolsheviks *(p.32)*.

Why did the Bolsheviks win the Russian Civil War?

There are 6 main reasons why the Bolsheviks *(p.32)* won:

- ✓ The Bolsheviks *(p.32)* had control of the industrial heartlands and transport links, which gave them a great advantage over their enemies. They had control over factories which made munitions.
- ✓ The Bolsheviks *(p.32)* had a strong, well-organised propaganda machine and used art, posters and entertainment to spread their message.
- ✓ They introduced conscription into the Red Army so they had five million soldiers by 1921.
- ✓ As commissar for war, Trotsky introduced harsh military discipline, recruited tsarist officers for their experience and used the agitprop trains to spread propaganda. He turned the Red Army into an effective force and his harsh discipline ensured loyalty to the Reds.
- ✓ The Red Terror *(p.67)* undermined opposition to the Bolsheviks *(p.32)* as the Cheka, or secret police, executed 50,000 of their enemies in 1918 including the tsar *(p.19)* and his family.
- ✓ Lenin's economic policy of War Communism took control of food production and manufacturing, which ensured the army was supplied.

Why did the Whites lose the Russian Civil War?

There were 6 key reasons why the Whites lost the civil war:

- ✅ They were reliant on foreign assistance for supplies and money, so the Whites were portrayed as the invading army.
- ✅ There was a severe lack of planning because they did not have one single leader as it was not a unified group.
- ✅ There were problems with communication, geographical distances and rivalry between the leaders.
- ✅ They were not united by a single goal as some wanted a return to tsarism, others favoured a military dictatorship and others preferred the Constituent Assembly *(p.62)*.
- ✅ The Whites did not control the major areas of industry, population or transport links because they tended to be on the outer edges of Russia.
- ✅ As a result their army was smaller and not as well supplied.

What were the consequences of the Russian Civil War?

There were 5 main consequences of the civil war.

- ✅ The Bolsheviks consolidated *(p.57)* their control over the country, economically with the policy of War Communism and politically as they destroyed their opposition using the Red Terror *(p.67)* and by winning the civil war.
- ✅ The policy of War Communism left the country economically ruined as food production and manufacturing collapsed.
- ✅ There was unrest with strikes and several different peasant uprisings, including the Tambov Uprising from 1920 to 1921, and the Kronstadt Uprising in 1921.
- ✅ Around eight million people died.
- ✅ The leaders of the Bolshevik *(p.32)* Party centralised control over their party as well as the country. All decisions were made by seven to nine key members of the Politburo *(p.70)* and orders were passed down to the rank and file.

DID YOU KNOW?

Power was centralised in the Politburo, the key decision-making body of the Communist Party.

THE RED TERROR

The Red Terror was a vicious attack on the opponents of the Bolsheviks.

What was the Red Terror?

The Red Terror was the Bolshevik-led *(p.32)* repression of their opposition during the Russian Civil War *(p.65)*.

When did the Red Terror in Russia happen?

The Red Terror officially lasted from September 1918 to 1920.

Who carried out the Red Terror?

The Red Terror was implemented by the Cheka, the Bolshevik *(p.32)* secret police force, led by Felix Dzerzhinsky.

Why was the Red Terror carried out?

There were 2 main reasons why the Red Terror happened:

- ✅ On 30th August 1918, Fanya Kaplan, a Socialist Revolutionary, attempted to assassinate Lenin because he shut down the Constituent Assembly *(p.62)* in January 1918.
- ✅ There was an attempted rebellion by the Socialist Revolutionaries in Moscow in July 1918.

What happened during the Red Terror?

The Red Terror involved 4 key events:

- ✅ Identifying, rounding up and arresting anyone suspected of 'counter-revolutionary' activities. In other words, anyone who was a threat to the Bolshevik *(p.32)* Party.
- ✅ The existing law courts were replaced by Revolutionary Tribunals. Officially, these were established to help the struggle against counter-revolutionary forces and defend the revolution.
- ✅ It is estimated that between 200,000 and 400,000 people died because of the Red Terror between 1918 and 1920.
- ✅ The party could force anyone to do hard labour and could execute anyone who resisted.

How did the Red Terror help the Bolsheviks win the Civil War?

The Red Terror helped the Bolsheviks *(p.32)* win the civil war in 4 main ways:

- ✅ It led to the execution of Tsar Nicholas II *(p.20)* and his family which removed the threat of the monarchy being restored to power.
- ✅ It removed many who opposed the Bolsheviks *(p.32)* and therefore weakened the opposition as a whole.
- ✅ It created fear and terror, which discouraged opposition.
- ✅ It was used to force the peasants to hand over grain during requisitioning, which ensured the Red Army was fed.

How many died during the Red Terror in Russia?

It's estimated that between 200,000 and 400,000 people were executed during the Red Terror between 1918 and 1920. Prison camps were also established on the Solovetsky Islands.

> **DID YOU KNOW?**
>
> The terror tactics the Cheka used were extreme and stories were told of people having their hands placed in boiling water.

THE KRONSTADT MUTINY, 1921

The Kronstadt Mutiny was a serious concern for Lenin as previously loyal sailors turned against the Communist Party.

What was the Kronstadt Naval Mutiny?

The Kronstadt Naval Mutiny, or the Kronstadt Uprising, was a revolt by sailors at the Kronstadt Naval base against the Bolsheviks *(p.32)* which was crushed by the Red Army.

When was the Kronstadt Naval Mutiny?

The Kronstadt Naval Mutiny happened between 28th February and 16th March, 1921.

Who was involved in the Kronstadt Naval Mutiny?

The sailors from the Kronstadt Naval base. Initially, sailors on the battleship Petropavlovsk mutinied. This spread to the whole naval base and about 15,000 sailors were involved.

What did the sailors demand in the Kronstadt Naval Mutiny?

The sailors made 4 key demands:
- New elections.
- Freedom of speech.
- Equal rations.
- The scrapping of the militia units which were taking grain from the peasants.

Why did the Kronstadt Naval Mutiny happen?

There were 6 main reasons why the Kronstadt Mutiny happened:
- War Communism was causing terrible suffering. The Bolsheviks *(p.32)* cut the bread ration by a third on 22nd January, 1921.
- On 23rd February, the Mensheviks and Social Revolutionaries organised a strike supported by workers from the local factories and shipyards.
- The Kronstadt sailors hated how Bolshevik *(p.32)* party leaders got special privileges, such as extra food.
- They objected to the Red Terror *(p.67)* as people were being arrested and executed without a fair trial.
- So, on 28th February, the crew of the ship Petropavlovsk mutinied because they felt the Bolsheviks *(p.32)* had drifted away from true communism.
- They wanted 'equal rations for all the working people' and 'freedom for the peasants'.

What happened during the Kronstadt Naval Mutiny?

There were 3 important events during the Kronstadt Naval Mutiny:
- The sailors on the battleship Petropavlovsk mutinied on 28th February, 1921.
- The sailors wrote a 15 point petition which included the demand for free elections to the soviets, equal rations and freedom of the press.
- There was a mass meeting of 15,000 sailors to discuss their demands and they adopted the slogan 'All power to the soviets - not to parties'.

What was the Bolsheviks response to the Kronstadt Naval Mutiny?

Lenin and the Bolsheviks *(p.32)* responded in 3 key ways:
- Initially, Lenin issued an ultimatum ordering the sailors to surrender, which they ignored.
- Trotsky organised attacks on the Kronstadt Naval base using 50,000 troops from Red Army and artillery. The Cheka were placed behind the Red Army troops and they shot any soldiers who retreated or refused to fire on the sailors.
- The Red Army had crushed the Kronstadt Mutiny by 17th March, 1921.

What were the results of the Kronstadt Naval Mutiny?

There were 5 key results of the Kronstadt Naval Mutiny:
- 10,000 Red Army soldiers were killed. 500 sailors were shot immediately and a further 2,000 were executed.
- About 4,000 were sent to Siberia to the gulags (labour camps) and about 8,000 fled to Finland.
- Lenin was very worried that previously loyal sailors had mutinied.
- As a result, he realised he needed to change his economic policy. He ended War Communism and brought in the New Economic Policy (NEP *(p.73)*).
- In March 1921, Lenin banned factions at the 10th Party Congress. He issued a decree, 'On Party Unity' which stated that factions were not allowed in the party - everyone had to support the policies of the party or they would be expelled from the party.

> **DID YOU KNOW?**
>
> The leader of the rebellion, Stepan Petrichenko, fled to Finland following the rebellion.

THE SOVNARKOM

The Sovnarkom was the cabinet of the Communist government.

What was the Sovnarkom?

The Sovnarkom was the Council of People's Commissars, also known as the SVK. It was established after the October Revolution *(p.56)* and focused on creating the USSR. It was the cabinet of the communist government made up of 13 to 20 People's Commissars. It issued the Bolsheviks *(p.32)* decrees.

Who was the leader of the Sovnarkom?

Lenin was the first chairman of the Sovnarkom.

When was the Sovnarkom formed?

The first Sovnarkom was created after the 1917 October Revolution *(p.56)*. When the Soviet Union was established, the Sovnarkom evolved to become its greatest executive or law-making authority.

How were the members of the Sovnarkom selected?

The members of the Sovnarkom were elected by the Central Executive Committee, which oversaw the work of the government. In reality, it consisted of the Communist Party's most powerful leaders from its central committee. In other words, the Sovnarkom was controlled by the Communist Party.

> **DID YOU KNOW?**
>
> The Sovnarkom met almost every day during the Russian Civil War

THE POLITBURO

The Politburo was the most important body of the Communist Party.

What was the Politburo?

The Politburo was part of the Communist Party of Russia and subsequently the Soviet Union. It consisted of 7 to 9 main members of the party. It was the highest policy-making authority in the party; they made all of the decisions.

When was the Politburo formed?

The Politburo was created in October 1917. From 1952 to 1966, it was renamed the Presidium.

Who were the first members of the Politburo?

Lev Kamenev, Vladimir Lenin, Joseph Stalin, Leon Trotsky and Grigory Zinoviev were the first members of the Politburo.

What was the power of the Politburo?

The Politburo was the most powerful body in the whole of the USSR. Its members made all key policy decisions, passing them to the other sections of the Communist Party and to the government through the Sovnarkom *(p.70)*.

How did Lenin use the Politburo?

Lenin used the Politburo to run the country. He did allow some debate and difference of opinion. During the Civil War, it took over decision-making from the central committee.

How did Stalin use the Politburo?

Under Stalin the Politburo lost its role as the central decision-making authority as he established a personalised dictatorship.

DID YOU KNOW?

Arkady Shevchenko, a Soviet diplomat famous for his defection to the USA, described the Politburo meetings as 'quiet, orderly, and methodical'.

WAR COMMUNISM, 1918-1921

War Communism was a very effective policy for helping the Bolsheviks win the civil war.

What was War Communism?

War Communism was an economic policy of the Bolsheviks *(p.32)* in which the state took control of the means of production, eg all factories, transport and farming. The government decided what was produced, when and by whom, and who would receive the goods.

When was War Communism introduced?

War Communism was introduced in June 1918 and ended in March 1921.

Who introduced War Communism?

Lenin and the Bolsheviks *(p.32)* introduced the policy of War Communism.

Why was War Communism introduced?

There were 4 important reasons why War Communism was brought in:

- ✅ The economy had collapsed due to the disruption caused by the First World War and the civil war, and the Bolsheviks *(p.32)* needed a way to deal with the shortages of food and goods.
- ✅ War Communism as a policy seemed to fit the communist theory as no one individual made a profit from their labour, the state controlled the means of production (the factories), and the state distributed produce according to the needs of the individual.

- The peasants were seen as resisting the Bolsheviks *(p.32)* by not supplying enough food for the cities, towns and the Red Army.
- The policy would ensure that the Red Army was supplied to fight in the civil war.

What were the aims of War Communism?

There were 3 key aims of the policy of War Communism:
- To gain control of the economy to enable them to win the war.
- To ensure enough supplies to resource the Red Army.
- To increase the Communist Party's control of the country.

What were the key features of War Communism?

There were 5 key features of War Communism:
- All industries were nationalised under the control of the Supreme Council of the Economy, or Vesenkha, in December 1917. Factories were set production targets.
- Military-style discipline was brought into the factories, which meant strikes were banned and there were harsh labour laws.
- Food rationing was introduced. Soldiers got the most, then workers, while the bourgeois and clergy received the least.
- Forced requisitioning of agricultural produce by 150,000 Bolsheviks *(p.32)*. There was strict price controls on all agricultural produce.
- All private trade was banned.

What were the positive effects of War Communism?

There were 2 important positive results of War Communism for the Bolshevik *(p.32)* Party:
- They were able to supply and feed the Red Army during the civil war which helped them to defeat the Whites and the Greens.
- They were able to centralise their control of the economy.

What were the negative effects of War Communism?

There were 7 important negative economic and social results of War Communism:
- Production levels collapsed even more. For example, coal production was 29 million tons in 1913 but by 1921 it was only 9 million.
- Food production collapsed to 48% of the 1913 productions levels. In 1913, 80 million tons of grain had been produced but in 1921, it was 37.6 million.
- There was an increase in violence and unrest in the countryside as peasants resisted food requisitioning. They hid their grain and slaughtered their animals rather than handing them over to the Bolsheviks *(p.32)*.
- By 1921, some regions faced famine. 29 million experienced famine and 5 million died.
- Workers from the cities and towns migrated to the countryside in search of food because there was less food in the towns.
- It resulted in peasant uprisings in 1920 and 1921, including the Tambov Uprising, and the Kronstadt Uprising by sailors in March 1921.
- A black market developed because of the shortages in goods and food.

> **DID YOU KNOW?**
>
> **In many ways, War Communism was an early version of a command economy.**
>
> The policy extended the Communist Party's control into all parts of the economy so they could direct resources to where they wanted them.

NEW ECONOMIC POLICY, 1921-1924

The New Economic Policy was a retreat from the government having complete control of the economy.

What was the NEP?

The New Economic Policy (NEP) was the Soviet government's economic policy. It represented a temporary retreat from its previous policy of War Communism.

When was the NEP introduced?

The New Economic Policy was introduced in 1921 and lasted until 1928.

Why was the NEP introduced?

There were 4 key reasons why the NEP was introduced:

- The previous economic policy of War Communism had resulted in economic collapse and famine in some areas of the USSR.
- War Communism had also resulted in massive unrest among the workers and the number of strikes increased.
- The peasants had risen up in protest against War Communism with one of the most serious revolts in Tambov, requiring 50,000 Red Army soldiers to crush it.
- The Kronstadt Mutiny in March 1921, by the sailors in the Kronstadt Naval base made the Bolsheviks *(p.32)* realise the dangers of continuing with the policy of War Communism.

How did the NEP work?

The NEP worked with 5 key features:

- Private ownership of businesses or banks that employed less than 20 people was allowed.
- Grain requisitioning from the peasants was stopped. Instead, they could sell it, keep the money and pay tax on anything they sold at a rate of 10%.
- The government kept control of heavy industry (coal, electricity, metal etc) and any large businesses.
- Money was reintroduced and so were some other aspects of the free market.
- People now had to pay taxes, first in goods and later in cash.

Who were the opponents of the NEP?

Some communists were disappointed with the NEP. They opposed it because they felt it betrayed their communist principles. Trotsky was one of those who opposed the NEP.

What were the positive effects of the NEP?

There were 5 key positive effects of the NEP:

- ☑ Grain production had increased by 50% by 1923.
- ☑ In 1922 the government introduced a new currency, called chervonets, which helped to stabilise the value of money.
- ☑ The prices of factory-made goods increased and there was greater demand for manufactured goods, especially from the countryside.
- ☑ There were fewer strikes and less discontent in the countryside.
- ☑ Trade with foreign countries increased, which helped the USSR financially.

What were the negative effects of the NEP?

There were 7 main negative effects of the NEP:

- ☑ Trade with other countries remained lower than that of 1913.
- ☑ Inequality also increased as some private business owners became richer. These were called NEPmen.
- ☑ Grain production increased, but it still wasn't enough to export large enough quantities abroad to get enough hard currency to fund industrialisation.
- ☑ Agriculture was still incredibly backwards.
- ☑ In 1923, there was the 'Scissors Crisis'. This was when food prices fell due to the supply of food increasing. However, the price of manufactured goods increased due to a shortage of manufactured goods. This made it difficult for peasants, who were earning less, and struggling to buy manufactured goods.
- ☑ Due to the Scissors Crisis the government forced the peasants to cut food prices. The peasants responded by feeding grain to their animals as meat was more expensive, meaning they made more money. By 1927, the amount of grain the government received decreased.
- ☑ Politically, Lenin came up against a lot of criticism as he was seen to have moved away from communist principles.

How did the NEP affect women?

In general, women's economic position worsened in 3 key ways as a result of the NEP.

- ☑ They were forced to give up their jobs for demobilised soldiers.
- ☑ The government did not see women's rights as a priority, and investment in the service industries was reduced.
- ☑ Following the revolution, gender equality only improved slightly.

Why was there opposition to the NEP?

There were 4 main reasons why different groups opposed the NEP:

- ☑ Some Bolsheviks (p.32) saw the NEP as a return to capitalism because it allowed people and small, privately owned businesses to make a profit. This was not acceptable to them and they believed the policy of War Communism was more aligned to their beliefs.
- ☑ The workers still suffered because of the increase in food prices, while unemployment increased and real wages only passed the 1914 level by 1928. In reality, workers were struggling to afford basic necessities.
- ☑ Some peasants were getting richer and there was growing inequality between the richer peasants called 'Kulaks' and ordinary peasants.
- ☑ Women were hit particularly hard as many were forced out of their jobs when the Red Army demobilised after the civil war and they ended up on the streets.

DID YOU KNOW?

Lenin said, 'Let the peasants have their little bit of capitalism as long as we keep power' about the NEP.

TSARINA ALEXANDRA

'Be more autocratic than Peter the Great and sterner than Ivan the Terrible.' Tsarina Alexandra commented to her husband, Tsar Nicholas II, in 1895.

Who was Tsarina Alexandra?

Alexandra Feodorovna was a German Princess who married Tsar Nicholas II *(p.20)* in 1894. She was unpopular at court.

What was Tsarina Alexandra famous for?

Tsarina Alexandra was famous for 4 key reasons:

- She was disliked at court, partly because she was German and Russia was at war with Germany during the First World War.
- When Nicholas II took personal command of the Russian Army in August 1915, he left Alexandra in charge of the government as his regent. She did a terrible job. She sacked capable ministers and replaced them with incompetent men.
- She allowed Rasputin to have too much influence over the running of the country.
- Her actions helped to increase opposition to tsarist rule, which in turn led to the February Revolution *(p.47)* 1917.

What was Tsarina Alexandra's relationship with Rasputin?

Tsarina Alexandra had a close relationship with Rasputin:

- She believed that Rasputin had mystical healing powers and could help her son, Alexei, who suffered from haemophilia.
- Rasputin had a great deal of influence over Tsarina Alexandra. Nicholas II made her regent in August 1915 because he had taken over personal command of the Russian Army during the First World War. Rasputin interfered with the appointments of ministers.
- There were rumours that Rasputin and Tsarina Alexandra were having an affair.

When did Tsarina Alexandra die?

Tsarina Alexandra and her family were executed by the Bolsheviks *(p.32)* on 17th July 1918, during the Russian Civil War *(p.65)*, to prevent the Whites and the Czech Legion from rescuing them.

DID YOU KNOW?

3 facts about Tsarina Alexandra:
- ✔ She was a German princess and the granddaughter of Queen Victoria.
- ✔ Her marriage to Nicholas was based on love.
- ✔ She had 5 children.

ALEXANDER KERENSKY

Alexander Kerensky was the second leader of the Provisional Government.

Who was Alexander Kerensky?

Alexander Kerensky was a member of the Socialist Revolutionary Party *(p.30)* in Russia and of the Provisional Government *(p.50)* between March 1917 and October 1917.

When was Alexander Kerensky important?
Kerensky became important between March 1917 and October 1917.

Why was Alexander Kerensky important?
Kerensky was important for 7 key reasons:
- He investigated the Lena Goldfield Massacre of 1912.
- He was elected as a member of the fourth Duma *(p.39)* as a delegate from the Trudovik Party. This was a party formed when some members of the Socialist Revolutionary Party *(p.30)* broke away because of the Party's decision to not take part in the first Duma *(p.36)*.
- He was appointed vice-chairman of the Petrograd Soviet *(p.49)*.
- He was made the Minister of War in May 1917, and organised the failed June Offensive *(p.52)* against Germany and Austria, which led to the July Days unrest.
- He appointed General Kornilov as the commander-in-chief of the Russian Army and had to use the Bolsheviks *(p.32)* to stop General Kornilov's attempted revolt in July 1917.
- He became the leader of the Provisional Government *(p.50)* in July 1917.
- He failed to stop the Bolsheviks *(p.32)* from overthrowing the Provisional Government *(p.50)* in October 1917.

When did Alexander Kerensky die?
Kerensky fled to America from Russia after the October Revolution *(p.56)* of 1917 and lived there until his death in 1970.

DID YOU KNOW?

Kerensky's father had taught Lenin at school.

GENERAL KORNILOV
General Kornilov was an experienced officer of both the Russo-Japanese War and the First World War.

Who was General Kornilov?
General Lavr Kornilov was a capable Russian general who served under the tsar *(p.19)* and the Provisional Government *(p.50)* during the First World War.

When was General Kornilov appointed to his role?
General Kornilov was appointed as commander-in-chief of Russian forces by the Provisional Government *(p.50)* in July 1917.

Why was General Kornilov appointed?
General Kornilov was appointed commander-in-chief to improve army discipline so Russia could win the First World War.

What was the role of General Kornilov?
General Kornilov had 3 main roles in the First World War:

- ✅ He was ruthless and opposed the Petrograd Soviet *(p.49)* and left-wing groups.
- ✅ He was suspected of trying to overthrow the Provisional Government *(p.50)* in July 1917 after he was ordered to bring troops to Petrograd to deal with the July uprising. This was known as the Kornilov affair.
- ✅ General Kornilov was sacked and the Provisional Government *(p.50)* lost the support of the army.

What were the results of General Kornilov's actions?

There were 2 main results of General Kornilov's actions in the Kornilov Affair:

- ✅ The Provisional Government *(p.50)* gave weapons to the Petrograd Soviet *(p.49)* to arm the Bolsheviks *(p.32)* to defend Petrograd against General Kornilov.
- ✅ He was arrested on 1st September, 1917.

How did General Kornilov die?

General Kornilov escaped and fought with the Whites during the civil war, in which he died.

DID YOU KNOW?

3 facts about General Kornilov:
- ✔ He believed in very strict military discipline. He wanted to bring back capital punishment.
- ✔ He was very conservative.
- ✔ He died in an explosion caused by a shell in Ekaterinodar.

VLADIMIR LENIN

Lenin was the first leader of the USSR, as well as its founder.

Who was Lenin?

Lenin was the leader of the Russian Communist Party and the USSR. He developed the political theory of Marxism-Leninism. His full name was Vladimir Ilyich Ulyanov.

When did Lenin join the Communist Party?

Lenin joined the Communist Party in 1903 and became the leader of the USSR after the October Revolution *(p.56)* of 1917 until his death in 1924.

Where was Lenin during the February Revolution?

Lenin was in exile in Switzerland. This meant he did not play a part in the February Revolution *(p.47)*.

When did Lenin return to Russia?

Lenin returned to Russia on 3rd April, 1917 but fled to Finland in July 1917. He returned again on 10th October, 1917.

Why did Lenin return to Russia?

Lenin was helped by the Germans to return to Russia. The Germans wanted to cause unrest in Russia in the hope the country would pull out of the First World War. They believed Lenin would cause that unrest.

What were Lenin's April theses?

Lenin's manifesto, his 'April Theses' had 4 main demands.
- ☑ Peace: He demanded that Russia pull out of the war.
- ☑ Bread: Lenin claimed the Bolsheviks *(p.32)* could solve the food shortages.
- ☑ Land: Lenin wanted land to be given to the peasants and to end the social hierarchies that had existed under the tsar. *(p.19)*
- ☑ All power to the Soviets: Lenin demanded all cooperation with the Provisional Government *(p.50)* and any other party should end, and all power should be with the Soviets.

What was Lenin's 'State and Revolution' pamphlet about?

The 'State and Revolution' pamphlet was:
- ☑ Written by Lenin while he was in Finland.
- ☑ Stated that after taking power in a revolution, there would be a period of rule known as the 'dictatorship of the proletariat'.
- ☑ Its aim would be to create stability in the nation before the transition to full communism.

What part did Lenin play in the Sovnarkom?

Lenin did the following on the Sovnarkom *(p.70)*, or the Council of People's Commissars:
- ☑ He was its chairman.
- ☑ He used the Sovnarkom *(p.70)* to develop a dictatorship, rather than Russia becoming a genuinely equal socialist society.

When did Lenin die?

Lenin died on 21st January 1924 after suffering three strokes; the first in May 1922, the second in December 1922 and the final one in March 1923.

Who were Lenin's potential successors?

After Lenin's death in 1924, there was a power struggle over who would succeed him:
- ☑ There were several potential leaders - Stalin, Trotsky, Kamenev, Zinoviev and Bukharin.
- ☑ Each candidate had their own strengths: Stalin was general secretary of the Communist Party, Trotsky had led the Red Army, and Zinoviev and Kamenev had led the party in Petrograd and Moscow.

Who succeeded Lenin?

By 1929, Stalin emerged as leader of the Communist Party and of the country.

How did Lenin's successor become leader?

There were 2 main methods Stalin used to become Lenin's successor:
- ☑ He manipulated his rivals, who were also competing to become leader of the party, so he was able to remove them as competitors.
- ☑ He appeared to be the most moderate candidate and rose above the arguments and egos of his rivals.

What were Lenin's achievements?

Lenin was the communist leader of Russia and the USSR between 1917 and 1924. He achieved 7 important things:
- ☑ He adapted Karl Marx's theory of communism to create Marxism-Leninism. This was a theory on how to achieve a communist society in Russia in a shorter period of time than Marxism would allow.

- ✓ He created the 'April Theses' which enabled the Bolsheviks *(p.32)* to get their message across more easily and gained them more support.
- ✓ He had led a successful communist revolution in Russia in October 1917.
- ✓ He led the Bolsheviks *(p.32)* to victory in the Russian Civil War *(p.65)*.
- ✓ He introduced War Communism which centralised Bolshevik *(p.32)* control of the economy, increased centralisation of the party and enabled them win the civil war.
- ✓ He ended Russia's war with Germany through the Treaty of Brest-Litovsk *(p.63)* in March 1918.
- ✓ He created a one-party state or a dictatorship.

DID YOU KNOW?

3 facts about Lenin:
- ✓ Lenin's older brother, Alexander, was executed for attempting to assassinate Tsar Alexander III.
- ✓ Lenin trained as a lawyer.
- ✓ Lenin's body was embalmed to preserve it and people can visit his mausoleum in Moscow's Red Square.

PRINCE LVOV

Prince Lvov was the head of the Provisional Government.

Who was Prince Lvov?

Prince Lvov was an aristocrat who was a liberal and Russian social reformer. He joined the Constitutional Democratic (Kadet) Party *(p.31)* in 1905 and was elected to the first Duma *(p.36)*. He became the first leader of the Provisional Government *(p.50)*.

When was Prince Lvov the leader of the Provisional Government?

Prince Lvov was the leader of the Provisional Government *(p.50)* between March and July 1917.

What did Prince Lvov do as leader of the Provisional Government?

As leader of the Provisional Government *(p.50)*, Prince Lvov continued with the war against Germany and had to resign after the July Days unrest.

DID YOU KNOW?

3 facts about Prince Lvov:
- ✓ He trained as a lawyer.
- ✓ He kept Russia in the First World War after the February Revolution of 1917.
- ✓ He moved to France after the October Revolution of 1917.

GRIGORI RASPUTIN

In 1905, Tsar Nicholas II said of Rasputin, 'He is just a good, religious, simple-minded Russian. When in trouble or assailed by doubts, I like to have a talk with him, and I invariably feel at peace with myself afterward.'

Who was Rasputin?

Grigori Rasputin was a Russian mystic who claimed he had healing powers. Some people thought he was a charlatan, but he became very powerful at the court of Tsar Nicholas II *(p.20)*.

When was Rasputin born?

Rasputin was born on 21st January, 1869.

How did Rasputin make it to the court?

Rasputin became a wanderer after he had a holy experience. He eventually found his way to the court of Nicholas II because he had a reputation as a healer.

What was Rasputin's role in the court?

Rasputin first became a healer for Alexei, son of Nicholas II and his wife, who had haemophilia. He also advised Tsarina Alexandra *(p.75)*.

Why was Rasputin controversial?

There were 4 key reasons why Rasputin was considered controversial:

- ✅ He started to accept bribes and sexual favours.
- ✅ Many believed he had an affair with Alexandra, the tsarina.
- ✅ Rasputin advised Alexandra over appointments to the government and interfered with political decisions during the First World War while the tsar *(p.19)* was at the frontline. People questioned how effective the government was, and how much influence Rasputin's had.
- ✅ The Tsarina would not listen to any criticism of Rasputin.

When was Rasputin murdered?

Rasputin was murdered in December 1916, by a group of aristocrats.

Why was Rasputin murdered?

Rasputin was murdered because he was hated by many members of the aristocracy as he was ruining the reputation of the royal family.

DID YOU KNOW?

Rasputin was assassinated.

He was poisoned, shot and then drowned because of his influence over Tsarina Alexandra played an important role in damaging the reputation of the royal family.

LEON TROTSKY

Leon Trotsky was the architect of the Red Army's success in the Russian Civil War.

Who was Trotsky?

Leon Trotsky was a Soviet revolutionary, Marxist theorist, and politician. Trotsky was a brilliant orator - he was much more charismatic than Stalin. He had worked closely with Lenin as the war commissar, commander of the Red Army.

Where was Trotsky during the February Revolution?

Trotsky had been in the USA during the February Revolution *(p.47)*. In May 1917, after the February Revolution, he returned to Russia.

What did Trotsky believe in?

Trotsky believed in 'permanent revolution'. His argument was that the revolution would degenerate if it could not spread and become international. He thought the Bolsheviks *(p.32)* should use instability around the world to spark revolutions elsewhere. This brought him into conflict with Stalin. Stalin believed in 'Socialism in One Country'.

What were Trotsky's main roles?

Trotsky had 4 key roles:

- He was elected president of the Petrograd Soviet *(p.49)* on 25th September 1917, because the Bolsheviks *(p.32)* had protected Petrograd from the Kornilov Revolt *(p.54)*.
- Trotsky played a key role in the October Revolution *(p.56)* in 1917, where he used the Military Revolutionary Committee to take over road bridges, telegraph offices and the army headquarters.
- Trotsky's was appointed as Commissar for War during the Russian Civil War *(p.65)*. In this role, he was responsible for the Red Army, and his actions were one of the key reasons the Bolsheviks *(p.32)* won.
- Trotsky negotiated the Treaty of Brest-Litovsk *(p.63)* with Germany which was signed on 3rd March, 1918.

What happened to Trotsky during the leadership struggle?

Stalin managed to remove Trotsky as a rival during the leadership struggle:

- Trotsky claimed Stalin deliberately told him the incorrect date for Lenin's funeral. This meant when Trotsky did not attend, his opponents could claim he did not respect Lenin's legacy.
- In 1924, Stalin allied with Zinoviev and Kamenev in supporting the New Economic Policy, in order to oppose Trotsky who wanted rapid industrialisation.
- Zinoviev and Kamenev worked against Trotsky at the Thirteenth Party Congress in 1924, so that all of Trotsky's ideas were rejected.
- Trotsky lost his job as Commissar for War in 1925.

What happened to Trotsky during the purges?

During the purges:

- Trotsky was not in the USSR during the Great Purges of 1936 to 1938 as he lived in exile.
- Other members of the Communist Party were accused of being 'Trotskyites', a threat to the USSR and communicating with Trotsky in their Show Trials.

How did Trotsky die?

Trotsky was murdered in Mexico on 20th August, 1940 by a member of the NKVD who forced an ice pick into his head.

DID YOU KNOW?

3 facts about Trotsky
- ✔ He was disliked by some members of the Communist Party who were anti-Semitic.
- ✔ He believed in 'permanent revolution'.
- ✔ He deserted his first family.

GLOSSARY

A

Abdicate - to give up a position of power or a responsibility.

Abolish, Abolished - to stop something, or get rid of it.

Abolition - the act of abolishing something, i.e. to stop or get rid of it.

Agricultural - relating to agriculture.

Agriculture - an umbrella term to do with farming, growing crops or raising animals.

Alliance - a union between groups or countries that benefits each member.

Allies - parties working together for a common objective, such as countries involved in a war. In both world wars, 'Allies' refers to those countries on the side of Great Britain.

Archaic - to be very old or old-fashioned.

Aristocracy - the highest social class, whose members gain their power from possessing land, property and money.

Aristocrat - a person who belongs to the aristocracy.

Artillery - large guns used in warfare.

Assassinate - to murder someone, usually an important figure, often for religious or political reasons.

Assassination - the act of murdering someone, usually an important person.

Assembly - a meeting of a group of people, often as part of a country's government, to make decisions.

Autocracy - a system of government where the ruler has absolute power over their country.

Autocrat - a ruler who has absolute power over their country.

B

Bolshevik, Bolsheviks - was a Russian radical Marxist revolutionary group, founded by Vladimir Lenin and Alexander Bogdanov in 1903. A Bolshevik is someone who is a member of that party.

Bourgeoisie - the capitalists who owned the means of production, i.e. land, banks and factories, in Marxist ideology.

Boycott - a way of protesting or bringing about change by refusing to buy something or use services.

Bribe, Bribery, Bribes - to dishonestly persuade someone to do something for you in return for money or other inducements.

C

Cabinet - politically, the group of senior ministers responsible for controlling government policy.

Capitalism - the idea of goods and services being exchanged for money, private ownership of property and businesses, and acceptance of a hierarchical society.

Ceasefire - when the various sides involved in conflict agree to stop fighting.

Censorship - the control of information in the media by a government, whereby information considered obscene or unacceptable is suppressed.

Civil rights - the rights a citizen has to political or social freedoms, such as the right to vote or freedom of speech.

Civilian - a non-military person.

Claim - someone's assertion of their right to something - for example, a claim to the throne.

Clergy - those ordained for religious duties, especially in the Christian Church.

Commune - a place where a group of people live and work together and share resources.

Communism - the belief, based on the ideas of Karl Marx, that all people should be equal in society without government, money or private property. Everything is owned by by the people, and each person receives according to need.

Communist - a believer in communism.

Conscription - mandatory enlistment of people into a state service, usually the military.

Conservative - someone who dislikes change and prefers traditional values. It can also refer to a member of the Conservative Party.

Consolidate - to strengthen a position, often politically, by bringing several things together into a more effective whole.

Constitution - rules, laws or principles that set out how a country is governed.

Constitutional - relating to the constitution.

Constitutional monarchy - political system in which a monarch's powers and authority are limited by a constitution.

Cooperate, Cooperation - to work together to achieve a common aim. Frequently used in relation to politics, economics or law.

Corrupt - when someone is willing to act dishonestly for their own personal gain.

Coup - a sudden, violent and illegal overthrow of the government by a small group - for example, the chiefs of an army.

Culture - the ideas, customs, and social behaviour of a particular people or society.

Currency - an umbrella term for any form of legal tender, but most commonly referring to money.

D

Debt - when something, usually money, is owed by a person, organisation or institution to another.

Decree - an official order with the force of law behind it.

Democracy - a political system where a population votes for its government on a regular basis. The word is Greek for 'the rule of people' or 'people power'.

GLOSSARY

Democratic - relating to or supporting the principles of democracy.

Dictatorship - a form of government where an individual or small group has total power, ruling without tolerance for other views or opposition.

Dictatorship of the Proletariat - the belief that, whilst the proletariat would eventually come to rule itself as proposed by Karl Marx, for now they were not ready, and required a 'dictator' to guide them until they were able to rule themselves.

Discriminate, Discrimination - to treat a person or group of people differently and in an unfair way.

Dispute - a disagreement or argument; often used to describe conflict between different countries.

Dissolution, Dissolve - the formal ending of a partnership, organisation or official body.

Divine right - the belief held by monarchs or rulers that they are given the right to rule by God.

E

Economic - relating to the economy; also used when justifying something in terms of profitability.

Economy - a country, state or region's position in terms of production and consumption of goods and services, and the supply of money.

Empire - a group of states or countries ruled over and controlled by a single monarch.

Estate, Estates - an extensive area of land, usually in the country and including a large house. It tends to be owned by one person, family or organisation.

Exile - to be banned from one's original country, usually as a punishment or for political reasons.

Export - to transport goods for sale to another country.

Extreme - furthest from the centre or any given point. If someone holds extreme views, they are not moderate and are considered radical.

F

Famine - a severe food shortage resulting in starvation and death, usually the result of bad harvests.

Foreign policy - a government's strategy for dealing with other nations.

Free elections - elections in which voters are free to vote without interference.

Front - in war, the area where fighting is taking place.

G

General strike - occurs when many different groups of workers strike at the same time, often with the aim of bringing a country to a standstill.

Gulag - a forced labour camp in the USSR.

H

Haemophilia - a genetic blood disorder where the blood does not clot properly.

Heavy industry - the manufacture of large and/or heavy items in bulk, or industries which involve large and heavy equipment and/or facilities. Examples are the iron, coal, steel and electricity industries.

Hierarchies, Hierarchy - the ranking of people according to authority, for example a colonel in the army being higher than a corporal.

I

Illiterate - unable to read or write.

Import - to bring goods or services into a different country to sell.

Independence, Independent - to be free of control, often meaning by another country, allowing the people of a nation the ability to govern themselves.

Industrial - related to industry, manufacturing and/or production.

Industrialisation, Industrialise, Industrialised - the process of developing industry in a country or region where previously there was little or none.

Industry - the part of the economy concerned with turning raw materials into into manufactured goods, for example making furniture from wood.

Inferior - lower in rank, status or quality.

Inflation - the general increase in the prices of goods which means money does not buy as much as it used to.

Infrastructure - the basic physical and organisational facilities a society or country needs to function, such as transport networks, communications and power.

International relations - the relationships between different countries.

L

Left wing - used to describe political groups or individuals with beliefs that are usually centered around socialism and the idea of reform.

Legitimacy, Legitimate - accepted by law or conforming to the rules; can be defended as valid.

Liberal - politically, someone who believes in allowing personal freedom without too much control by the government or state.

M

Manifesto - the stated policies or aims of a political party or person, normally published before an election.

Massacre - the deliberate and brutal slaughter of many people.

GLOSSARY

Means of production - resources which enable the production of goods, such as tools, factories and raw materials.

Merchant, Merchants - someone who sells goods or services.

Middle class - refers to the socio-economic group which includes people who are educated and have professional jobs, such as teachers or lawyers.

Military force - the use of armed forces.

Militia - an army created from the general population.

Minister - a senior member of government, usually responsible for a particular area such as education or finance.

Mir - was a village in which the community holds the land jointly but farms it individually in tsarist Russia.

Mobilisation - the action of a country getting ready for war by preparing and organising its armed forces.

Moderate - someone who is not extreme.

Modernise - to update something to make it suitable for modern times, often by using modern equipment or modern ideas.

Monarchists - people in favour of living in a country governed by a monarchy.

Monarchy - a form of government in which the head of state is a monarch, a king or queen.

Morale - general mood of a group of people.

Mutiny - a rebellion or revolt, in particular by soldiers or sailors against their commanding officers.

Mystical - relating to magical, religious or spiritual powers.

N

Nationalism, Nationalist, Nationalistic - identifying with your own nation and supporting its interests, often to the detriment or exclusion of other nations.

Nobility - the social class ranked directly below royalty.

Noble, Nobles - another word for aristocrat - a member of the highest and richest class in society.

O

Oath - a solemn promise with special significance, often relating to future behaviour or actions.

Occupation - the action, state or period when somewhere is taken over and occupied by a military force.

P

Parliament - a group of politicians who make the laws of their country, usually elected by the population.

Patriotic - a strong love of and support for one's country.

Peasant - a poor farmer.

Police state - a totalitarian country in which the police have a great deal of power to control the people and suppress opposition.

Population - the number of people who live in a specified place.

Poverty - the state of being extremely poor.

President - the elected head of state of a republic.

Prevent, Preventative, Preventive - steps taken to stop something from happening.

Production - a term used to describe how much of something is made, for example saying a factory has a high production rate.

Profit - generally refers to financial gain; the amount of money made after deducting buying, operating or production costs.

Propaganda - biased information aimed at persuading people to think a certain way.

Prosecute - to institute or conduct legal proceedings against a person or organisation.

Prosperity - the state of thriving, enjoying good fortune and/or social status.

Province, Provinces - part of an empire or a country denoting areas that have been divided for administrative purposes.

Purged, Purging - abrupt and often violent removal of a group of people from a place or organisation; medically, to make someone sick or induce diarrhoea as a treatment to rid them of illness.

R

Radical, Radicalism - people who want complete or extensive change, usually politically or socially.

Rationing - limiting goods that are in high demand and short supply.

Real wages - a person's income in terms of how much they can buy after taking inflation into account.

Rebellion - armed resistance against a government or leader, or resistance to other authority or control.

Rebels - people who rise in opposition or armed resistance against an established government or leader.

Reform, Reforming - change, usually in order to improve an institution or practice.

Regent - the person who rules when the king is away, incapacitated or too young to rule.

Reign - a period of power, usually by a monarch.

Relief - something that reduces pressure on people, often through financial or practical support.

Reparations - payments made by the defeated countries in a war to the victors to help pay for the cost of and damage from the fighting.

Repress, Repression - politically, to prevent something or control people by by force.

Repressive - a harsh or authoritarian action; usually used to describe governmental abuse of power.

GLOSSARY

Republic - a state or country run by elected representatives and an elected/nominated president. There is no monarch.

Requisition - to take something, usually by official order, such as a government taking food from peasants.

Revolution - the forced overthrow of a government or social system by its own people.

Right wing - a political view with beliefs centred around nationalism and a desire for an authoritarian government opposed to communism.

Riots - violent disturbances involving a crowd of people.

Russification - a policy implemented by the tsars in Russia to enforce Russian culture and language on non-Russian ethnic groups.

S

Self-determination, Self-determined - in politics, the process where a nation decides its own statehood and whether it will rule itself rather than be part of a larger empire.

Serfdom - the condition or state of being a serf.

Socialism - a political and economic system where most resources, such as factories and businesses, are owned by the state or workers with the aim of achieving greater equality between rich and poor.

Socialist - one who believes in the principles of socialism.

Soviet - an elected workers' council at local, regional or national level in the former Soviet Union. It can also be a reference to the Soviet Union or the USSR.

State, States - an area of land or a territory ruled by one government.

Strike - a refusal by employees to work as a form of protest, usually to bring about change in their working conditions. It puts pressure on their employer, who cannot run the business without workers.

Subsistence, Subsistence farming, Subsistent - a type of farming in which farmers only grow or produce enough for their own use, with no surplus to sell.

Successor - someone who succeeds the previous person, such as a leader who takes over the role from the previous holder.

Suppress, Suppression - the use of force to stop something, such as a protest.

T

Tactic - a strategy or method of achieving a goal.

Territories, Territory - an area of land under the control of a ruler/country.

Trade unions - organised groups of workers who cooperate to make their lives better at work. For example, they might negotiate for better pay and then organise a strike if one is refused.

Treaty - a formal agreement, signed and ratified by two or more parties.

Tsar - the Russian word for emperor; can also be spelled 'czar'.

U

Ultimatum - a final demand, with the threat of consequences if it is not met.

Upper class - a socio-economic group consisting of the richest people in a society who are wealthy because they own land or property.

V

Veto - the right to reject a decision or proposal.

W

Welfare - wellbeing; often refers to money and services given to the poorest people.

Working class - socio-economic group consisting of those engaged in waged labour, especially manual work or industry, who typically do not have much money.

Z

Zemstvos - elected local assemblies, set up Russia in 1864 to administer local affairs.

INDEX

B
Bloody Sunday, 1905 - 26
Bolsheviks - 32
Bolsheviks, War Communism - 71
Bolsheviks, consolidation of power - 57
Bolsheviks, growth of support - 55

C
Civil War, Russian - 65
Communist Party in Russia - 64
Constituent Assembly - 62

D
Declaration of the Rights of the Peoples of Russia. - 62
Decree on Nationalities - 61
Decrees on Workers' Rights - 60
Discontent, tsarist Russia - 23
Duma - 36

F
February Revolution - 47
Feodorovna, Alexandra - 75
First Duma - 36
Fourth Duma - 39
Fundamental Laws - 35

J
July Days, Russia - 53
June Offensive - 52

K
Kadet Party - 31
Kerensky, Alexander - 75
Kornilov Revolt - 54
Kornilov, General - 76
Kronstadt Naval Mutiny - 68

L
Land Decree - 59
Lena Goldfield Strike - 43
Lenin, Vladimir - 77
Lvov, Georgy - 79

M
Manifesto on the Improvement of the State Order - 34
Menshevik Party - 33

N
New Economic Policy (NEP) - 73

O
October Manifesto - 34
October Revolution - 56
Octobrist Party - 29
Opposition to Tsar Nicholas II - 24

P
Peace Decree - 59
Petrograd Soviet - 49
Politburo - 70
Prince Lvov - 79
Provisional government, establishment - 50

R
Rasputin, Grigori - 80
Red Terror - 67
Russia and WW1 - 44
Russia, early 1900s - 16
Russia, impact of WW1 - 46
Russian Civil War - 65
Russian Revolution, 1905 - 27
Russian calendar - 18
Russification - 42
Russo-Japanese War - 25

S
Second Duma - 37
Social Democratic Party - 32
Socialist Revolutionary Party - 30
Sovnarkom - 70
Stolypin, Pyotr - 40
Stolypin, land reforms - 41

T
Third Duma - 38
Treaty of Brest-Litovsk - 63

Get our free app at GCSEHistory.com

INDEX

Trotsky, Leon - *81*
Trudoviks Party - *30*
Tsar Nicholas II - *20*
Tsar Nicholas II, opposition - *24*
Tsarina Alexandra - *75*
Tsarist Russia, discontent - *23*
Tsarist police state - *22*
Tsars - *19*

W

War Communism, Bolshevik - *71*
Winter Palace, storming of - *57*

Milton Keynes UK
Ingram Content Group UK Ltd.
UKHW050845280224
438592UK00005B/53